Sand Walker

A lifetime on Morecambe Bay

CEDRIC ROBINSON

Foreword by
ALASTAIR BRUCE OF CRIONAICH

GREAT NORTHERN

To my wife, Olive, my family and to the many, many friends
we have made over our years here at Guide's Farm

Uniform with this volume
SAND PILOT OF MORECAMBE BAY by Cedric Robinson

Great Northern Books
An imprint of Atlantic Publishers,
Holebottom Farm, Hebden, Skipton, BD23 5DL

ISBN: 0 9535035 5 0

© Cedric Robinson 2000
Line drawings by Olive Robinson
08378672
Design, layout and reproduction: Barnabus Design & Repro, Truro

Printed by The Amadeus Press Ltd, Bradford

British Catlaoguing in Publication Data
A catalogue record for this book is available from the British Library

∾ CONTENTS ∾

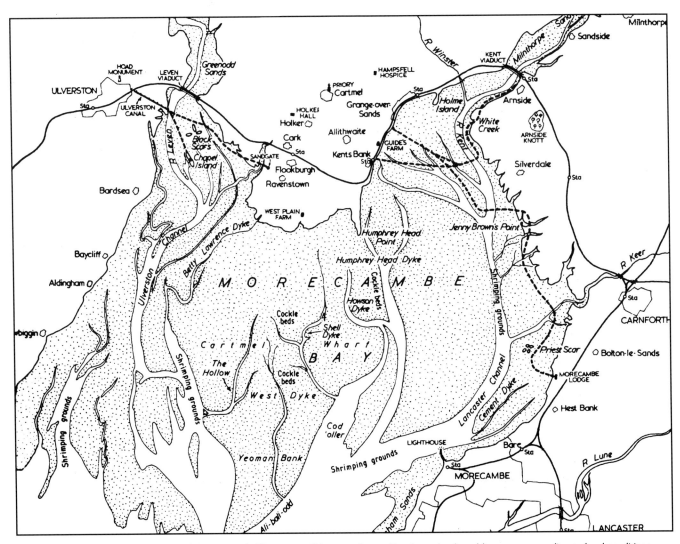

The Morecambe Bay area and its fishing grounds. The routes of the cross-Bay walks, shown by dotted lines, vary according to local conditions.

~ FOREWORD ~

CEDRIC ROBINSON first introduced me to the inviting but treacherous sands of Morecambe Bay in his capacity as The Queen's Guide over Kent Sands. His appointment is an ancient one, born of need and thus nurtured by abbots and sovereigns since the Middle Ages, for the service of travellers wishing to negotiate the shifting sands and speeding tides that hamper this tempting short cut. As this book explains, this assistance is still provided to thousands each year by a remarkable man: both young and old follow Cedric's sure-footed guidance through the danger of nature's ever-changing tricks and devices.

One of those who Cedric guided to cross the bay was the Duke of Edinburgh and it was he who encouraged me to include the Guide's unique appointment in the book *Keepers of the Kingdom*, which I wrote to explain the rich history behind the ancient titles that survive today.

Born to these sands, Cedric's enthusiasm for the place overflows the post he holds. His passion is matched by the support he gets from his wife, Olive, without whom his lifetime of Guiding and giving could not have flourished. It is their love for both life and the powerful characteristics of their marine environment that fills these pages. All of us who have walked these unpredictable sands with the Robinsons, learning with each step, will enjoy the memories he provokes. Those who have yet to make the journey will be inspired to do so at his side. By calling on the services of The Queen's Guide over Kent Sands, they will be continuing a centuries old tradition, as valid now as it ever was.

ALASTAIR BRUCE OF CRIONAICH

CEDRIC ROBINSON

Just like St Christopher,
Guard of the Sands,
Knows every channel
Like the back of his hands.

Unlike the voyagers
Of Dick Turpin's day,
The traveller's safe
Across Morecambe Bay.

And the branches he plants
In this muddy expanse
Are a symbol of safety
That are seen at a glance.

And he writes books
On his tales of the sand
So Morecambe is heard of
All over the land.

Rubs shoulders with dukes,
Wears his title with pride –
Cedric Robinson
The Morecambe Bay Guide!

WILLIAM MACLEAN – AGED 12

SANDS GUIDE

In 1963 I was officially appointed as the 25th Guide over Morecambe Bay sands to be installed at Guide's Farm since the first Royal Appointment. The early learning given to me by my Dad stood me in good stead for this important work. It was totally different from the job I had been used to as a fisherman and although I was still able to continue with fishing, I would now be dealing with people as well and was looking forward to this.

I have a lovely wife Olive and when we moved to Guide's Farm we had a much younger family of three boys and two girls. I was very proud of them all. Bill, the eldest son worked on the sands with me for a while after leaving school and later, after meeting his future wife Jacqui who lived in Barrow, moved there later to work for his father-in-law, Mr Tom Ward. Bill has a son and daughter who are adults now, and one lovely grandchild. He runs his own thriving family business at Barrow-in-Furness. Bill has been very involved with promoting wind-surfing round the coast.

Guide's Farm was called Carter House at one time and many of the earlier guides used that name. The house was very old and damp but it was built to last with walls at least three feet deep and the ceilings were heavily beamed, probably being made from old ships' timbers. Low doorways and sloping floors added to the character of the place. The railway embankment now acts as a seawall in front of the house but in days gone by high tides could swill into the downstairs rooms.

Thirty-seven years ago Cartlane was a very quiet place and although a public footpath ran straight past the front gate of the farm, we hardly ever saw a soul from one week to the next.

Neighbours were few but that did not bother us as we always seemed to be so busily occupied at work, if not on the sands then in the large living-room with the table in the centre, an oilcloth covering the table and a huge heap of Morecambe Bay shrimps in the centre with the family sitting round picking or shelling the shrimps. At weekends and in school holidays we always had a houseful of children who became quite good at picking shrimps and earned themselves a bit of pocket money.

It was always a happy house but it seemed to be all work and no play for Olive as she had all the cleaning up to do and the washing down afterwards. This always was and still is her way; she will never ever go to bed even now and leave an untidy house or a pot unwashed. I always got up next morning to see everything clean and in place.

In those days the cross bay walks were not as popular as they are today as they were taking place at weekends usually, but only on Sundays. No-one wanted a Saturday walk as most people worked until Saturday lunchtime then. Most of the walks started out from Hest Bank and took no longer than three hours, coming ashore at the Grange side of the bay at Grange-over-Sands railway station or sometimes at the Bathing Pool, whichever was the most suitable at the time.

Thirty-five years ago at the age of five years Clifford Law came to visit us from Leeds for the first time, bringing with him the excitement of a city child in one big adventure and to experience the fascinating yet busy life-style of Guide's Farm.

In July, 1964 the train pulled into Kents Bank station and young Clifford stepped down from the train. He was with his Nanny and Grandpa Haley, Olive's and Clifford's mother's parents. I was unkown to Clifford so I introduced myself as Uncle Ced, but Clifford's thoughts were about meeting his new cousins who lived at Guide's Farm overlooking the sea. As we left the station they all climbed into my little mini-van, Nanny installed in the front with me and Grandpa and Clifford in the back. As we approached, we started to descend Carter Road with Clifford peering excitedly between the two front seats and through the windscreen at the beautiful view of the bay.

I pulled up alongside the gateway to the top field to get a better view, then as we made our way down the hill he became more excited as he still does now when he comes to Grange. This is not surprising as it is such a wonderful place. Clifford was about to meet the most loving, good-natured person in the world he could ever wish to know – his Aunty Olive.

She greeted him with a cuddle and a kiss and Clifford knew from that day he would like it here. He then met Paul, his cousin – two shy lads with the same mixed, confused thoughts. Would they get on together? Well they did and have built up a relationship to this present day as cousins and best friends.

Neither Olive nor I seemed to get much leisure time, if any at all, but I was always drawn to Morecambe when I was a teenager and dearly loved to go there in earlier times with my father and visit Morecambe Trawlers Ltd. where we bought our ropes, fishing nets, shrimp and fluke nets etc. I just loved the place so when the opportunity arose and enabled Olive and me to take an evening off with the children as a trip out to Morecambe lights and Happy Mount Park, everyone was delighted.

That summer Clifford's Mum and Dad had asked Olive and I if we would look after Clifford and his two sisters, Janet and Andrea for a fortnight while they went on their second honeymoon and we could not see any problem – just another three kids in a full house already!

Setting off from the farm I drove with Olive sitting next to me in the front of the van, Dianne our eldest daughter, Jean the youngest of our family, Janet, Andrea, Paul and Clifford all sat crouched up in the back – nowadays it would have been illegal but not then. It probably seemed a long way for the children, but with my singing and whistling "Seven little girls sitting in the back seat, everyone in love with Ced" the time soon passed very happily.

The approach into Morecambe from the children's point of view was "Wow" – look at all these fairy lights flashing on and off. So many different colours and shapes.

Clifford had experienced a very different view from Paul's bedroom window at the farm, but now he was seeing it all, right in front of him. We managed to find a space to park on the sea front and everyone climbed out of the van full of excitement.

"Where can we go first? What can we do? Look at that? were the cries from six kids who were longing to make this visit last as long as possible. We all held hands for safety and crossed the road together. The amusement arcades were smack, bang in front of us. The music and noise the machines made were electrifying. The children stood in amazement at first but they all had some spending money and really enjoyed these slot machines.

We thought it would be a good idea to take them to Happy Mount Park, which was some distance from where we were, so we started walking back along the seafront until we reached a long queue of people waiting at the entrance to the Park. We could see clearly through the main gates that the whole of the Park was alive with lights and moving animated characters with people following the routed path of a wonderland fantasy trip. It was breathtaking, like a huge maze which no-one wanted to get out of.

When we had done the full tour we headed back to the car, stopping for fish and chips on the way before driving back home to Grange.

We arrived back at Guide's Farm, everyone tired out but very happy with the experience and went upstairs to bed, looking out of the bedroom window across the bay at the string of lights in the distance and thinking we have been there, wasn't it fun – lights out now and into bed.

Although I was still kept busy on the sands with the

(Top) An early photograph of Guide's Farm, with the guide on horseback.

(Lower) Grange-over-Sands in 1900, before the channel of the Kent moved to the opposite side of the Bay. Claire House Pier is long gone. (A.N. Wolstenholme collection − 2).

fishing and the walks at weekends, it is said of fishing that the real work only starts once you get home, which I am sure is true. Olive and I decided that it would be a good idea to buy some pigs – two in fact, from a farmer who lived way out in the country from Grange-over-Sands on the A65, not far from Giggleswick in Yorkshire. We saw the advertisement in our local newspaper – The Westmorland Gazette. I had a new recruit at Guide's Farm called Ziggy. He had come straight from school, a tall, lanky and very willing young lad but Paul and Clifford were not as tall and I think were a bit envious of Ziggy. Paul had an early morning paper round to do but with Clifford's help they could get round quicker and they wanted to be back in time to collect the pigs.

6.30 am. I shouted upstairs. "Time you were up lads, your breakfast is waiting". "What are we doing today"? "If you hurry up with your paper round you can come with me and Ziggy to pick up some lile piglets from this farmer I know but I have to collect Ziggy first". That morning Paul and Clifford must have flown round with the papers as they returned here at the farm before me. Paul and Clifford sat in the back of the van while Ziggy took the front passenger seat with me driving. They did not seem to mind being in the back while we sat up't front in comfort.

When we arrived at the farm we had a look round before selecting our pigs with Ziggy giving orders of what to do and where to go when all of a sudden a Gurt big dog jumped out at him – luckily the dog was on a chain – but it certainly took us by surprise and frightened us at the time.

I chose my pigs from a large litter, paid the farmer his dues and then we were off returning home. There were quite a number of gates to open on our way to the farm so obviously it was the same going back. As Ziggy was in the front of the van, the job of opening and shutting the gates fell to him. Now – Paul and Clifford thought it would be rather amusing if every time Ziggy got out to open the gates we would drive off without him. Quite naughty really – making him walk to the next gate! When we did

get on our journey the piglets were beginning to take it in turn to mess and pee in the back of the van whilst Paul and Clifford had to sit with them.

The minute we returned to Guide's Farm the boys could not wait to get out – it stunk. They deserved it really though when they made Ziggy walk between the gates to the farm!

The pig sty had been prepared previously for the piglets so they were shoved into their new home whilst I now drove the van up onto some ramps I had to hose it down inside and make it smell fresh and clean again.

We were now almost self-sufficient at Guide's Farm. We caught and ate our own fish, grew our own potatoes and fresh vegtables – carrots, turnips and beetroot. By purchasing the piglets we intended to fatten them – one would be for our own use for the family at the farm and the other would be given to the butcher at Flookburgh in exchange for taking them to the slaughter-house to be humanely killed. Then he brought one back to the farm ready cut up – one half for meat which we put in the freezer and the other half, bacon and hams, were cured in the old-fashioned way by rubbing salt into them on a cold slab and they were put in muslin eventually and hung from hooks in the beams on the stairs. Olive, my wife made some lovely brawn from the pigs heads – quite a task but well worth the bother. She would often buy a rabbit from the butcher and make a lovely rabbit pie which was much enjoyed by us all.

Now we had rabbits on our doorstep, up in the fields, and they were a menace to the greencrop of carrots, white turnips etc. so something had to be done. It seems cruel to think of it now and there was no way I could harm wildlife even if it was a pest – I am too soft-natured – but it was a case of survival, nature's way of keeping pests at bay on the farm which was self-sufficient.

I have always kept a dog, even as a small boy and now I had two fine lurchers, Yogi and Cindy, which were kept in a large kennel at the back of the barn. Yogi was jet black, well-built and a very clever dog. Cindy came later but they were good company for each other. Paul and Clifford kept asking when could they go rabbiting. This depended on the weather and after we had had our tea one day, the lads were forever going outside to check and then they would come back in and say to me "It looks all right". I asked them to settle down as we would not be going anywhere yet – it was still too light. "You'll have to wait till the sun goes down and dusk sets in when I can get the van out".

Clifford wondered what on earth we were going to do with the van, so I said "Tha'l see 'mi' lad". A little while later on "Is it dark enough yet? Come on then, lets go, can we get the dogs?" "No!" Robert had just arrived and he got the dogs and I said that we would get the van.

Paul and Clifford followed me into the yard and I asked Paul to open the yard gates and then they climbed into the back of the van. Meanwhile Robert had arrived with Cindy and Yogi, so he opened the back doors of the van and let the dogs jump in with Paul and Clifford. Clifford could not get over the size of Yogi – he was big and bold and could jump over a five-barred gate and scale most hedges – in fact he was a very fit dog. They sat down in the back but were very alert, wagging their tails, then strutting backwards and forwards, heads turning left and right, quicker than the boys had ever seen anything move before.

I drove up into the top field without lights, just being able to make out where we were going. The lads asked me why was I driving up in the field in the dark. "You'll see in a minute" and as I pulled up Robert got out quickly. "Can we get out?" Clifford asked me. I told him to wait a minute until Robert had sorted out the dogs. The van doors were opened and both dogs jumped out with Rob hanging on to them with leashes.

I asked the boys to get out now but to keep quiet and stay behind Rob. I then switched the headlights on and Rob let Yogi off the leash. The dog then shot off like an arrow until he picked up the scent. He then broke into a trot, sniffing around the edge of the field, his head moving from side to side staring into the dark when he froze

suddenly for a split second and then set off into a racing gallop.

The light from the van caught a glimpse of a rabbit shooting across the field but close on its heels was Yogi. Then Robert let Cindy loose and she went straight into action and both dogs were circling round a cluster of small trees and bushes. The dogs now resembled kangaroos, jumping about on all fours and doing all this thudding confuses the rabbits and they break out into the open. That night we, or should I say the dogs, caught four rabbits and I skinned them and gave Paul and Clifford a rabbit tail apiece for good luck. On this occasion the rabbits were taken to Grange to the local butcher in part exchange for Olive's meat order.

At the Kents Bank end of our fields was a big house with only the footpath separating it from the railway line. I can just remember that there were three or four elderly ladies living there with lots of cats. The name of the people was the Misses Barwick and they were hardly ever seen but when they died eventually I was asked for permission for a marquee to be erected in our fields. This was to contain the items for sale and it was almost like an antique fair. Olive walked along to the sale with our nearest neighbours, Eva and Jack Burrow who lived at Cartlane railway crossings. They said the sale was very interesting with lots of antiques but they did not buy anything.

About this time we were to have new neighbours who were retiring into Grange-over-Sands from Beardwood, near Blackburn. Mr & Mrs Hirst called on us and said they had purchased a plot of land a short distance from us in Carter Road. They were to have a bungalow built and wondered if I would have time to help with levelling the ground and laying out the garden and of course I agreed.

As time moved on Mrs Hirst became very fond of our two youngest children Paul and Jean. Their own family, a son and daughter, had grown up and been away from home for some time. What lovely people they turned

Cedric inspects the rare sight of ice on the Bay in the hard winter of 1982. The route out to the sands was blocked for two weeks. (Paul Nickson) out to be – really sincere friends. They had a corgi called Sandy whom they thought the world of and enjoyed the lovely quiet walks we have in this area, accompanying them around Kents Bank and Grange. Mrs Hirst would bake her speciality 'Parkin' every week and bring some round for us at the farm. Each bonfire night we invited them, they loved Guides Farm, our company and that of the young children. Very sadly, Mrs Hirst met with a tragic accident on the railway line at Kents Bank Station. We were absolutely devasted here at the farm feeling numb for days on end and could not concentrate on anything with this dreadful accident on our minds. Mr Hirst, her widower, left the area and went to live in Yorkshire.

A neighbour of the Hirsts living in a cottage along Cartlane was a Miss Wray and this cottage backed on to Mr & Mrs Hirst's bungalow. This lady was a well-built, middle-aged person and was a great character. I understand she had been a Matron (Nurse) and was very clever, but never a day went by without her making her daily walk passing the farm with her dog which looked like a wire-haired terrier but very much overweight, and her cat- black and white - an enormous size for a cat. It was fun to see them going walkies together.

When Miss Wray stopped at our house to pass the time of day it was very noticeable that the cat would paw at the dog in such a way which we had never seen before. It was quite amusing, as if to say come on let's get moving.

One day Miss Wray came to the farm in a very upset state as her cat had not come home the previous night and she was so worried she asked me to look out for it around the farm.

Later that day I spotted it when I was looking after the cattle at the top of our fields. The huge cat was up one of the old ash trees so I came home immediately and rang Miss Wray who came along right away. I suggested driving my tractor up the fields and also took a ladder.

We got the tractor as close to the tree as possiible and then placed the ladder from the tractor on to the branch where the cat was sitting. I thought to myself "We'll soon have her down" but just as I reached out for her she climbed further up the tree, higher and higher, almost to the top and we did not know what to do so decided to come back down to the farm. Miss Wray went home and I said that I would have another look up in the fields later to see if anything more had happened before it was dark. Meanwhile, Miss Wray was so frantic when the cat was still up in the tree the next morning that she rang the Grange-over-Sands fire-brigade and in no time at all they were on their way.

It was impossible to get the vehicle across my fields so this was left on Carter Road, near to the top gateway and the firemen carried a long ladder to the ash tree. They managed to reach the cat and retrieved it fairly quickly – although I think it gave itself up – and was none the worse for the adventure. I do think that Miss Wray received a bill for expenses incurred at the time, as she did call the firemen out to the rescue.

Miss Wray was certainly a character and one would not want to get on the wrong side of her. She told us once that as she was taking her cat and dog for a walk along the footpath past our field towards Kents Bank a young cyclist came along like a bat out of hell (her own words). She shouted at him to slow down as this was a footpath. He just sneered at her and cycled on. After a while he returned but this time Miss Wray was ready for him – she put her stick through his front wheel and sent him sprawling!

Yes, Cartlane was a very interesting place to live and we were meeting people and making new friends all the time.

Paul's best friends were Peter and Brian Fishwick of Cartlane. Mr and Mrs Wells kept the Post Office and general stores at the top of Cartlane.

Dick and Marjorie Burrows lived 'up the orchard'. Dick was a keen fisherman who loved the sands and he was always working. He also loved his hobby of hound-trailing. His younger brother Gren and his wife May are very near neighbours of ours and have become close friends since they retired.

Fred Broomfield became friends with us 36 years ago. His younger brother John, who used to have the old nurseries farm in Cartlane emigrated to New Zealand. John and Andree with their two daughters, Wendy and Julie, and their little son Ian moved to Matamata in New Zealand in 1965 and were sadly missed as they were all friends of ours and the children. They now have another son, Simon who was born in New Zealand. Fred lived in Kents Bank with his elderly parents and when he retired from the Merchant Navy as a Chief Radio Officer and after his parents died, he often visited us here at Guide's Farm. He has been coming here for so long that he is treated as one of the family. Fred is a very sincere person with a heart of gold and he still comes down to the shore with Olive when the walks come in to Kents Bank and helps in supplying the books and certificates.

Another very good friend is Mrs Alexander, who lives across the field from us. She always takes an interest in the bay and the walks, and shows a keen concern for animals generally but particularly in our goats. Mrs Alexander always looks out for them and usually brings some titbit for their pleasure.

As our daughter Jean got older, she was so soft-natured and sensitive we were no longer allowed to chase after rabbits at night and we never had any pigs again at Guide's Farm – although we still managed to grow some very good carrots!.

As time moved on we were getting much busier at the farm and out on the sands. The number of people who visited us or phoned on a day to day basis was unbelievable.

I was asked if I would be interested in joining her Majesty's Coastguard service as an auxiliary. My colleagues were based at Arnside with the main headquarters at Liverpool. I agreed to join as I thought it would be a useful asset. My application was accepted and I was enrolled as a member on 31st August 1977. Eventually I was given a powerful VHF radio which I always carry with me while out in the bay, in case I am needed in an emergency.

When one has learned the dangers of the bay from a very early age one respects them and does not venture out on the sands without full knowledge of the prevailing conditions. However, for the safety of the holiday-makers, a siren or hooter is sounded to warn them of the dangers of the incoming tide. I always have powerful binoculars and during the summer season regularly scan the bay for unwary walkers, but occasionally accidents do happen.

Almost every household in Grange and Kents Bank has an excellent view across the estuary and if anyone out there is seen to be in danger residents should ring 999 immediately and ask for the Coastguard to report the incident. The Coastguards are the people who have the most knowledge and they also have the right equipment for any rescue and they generally have this equipment available immediately. The Fire Brigade and rescue services around the bay from Silverdale to Fleetwood are seeking to update their equipment for such rescues from the muddy shores, rivers, gullies, marsh and quicksands of Morecambe Bay and beyond so if they are called out to rescue in mud or quicksands they will have the means to deal with these difficult accidents in as fast a time as possible and help to save lives. The time of the tides must always be in the forefront of their minds before leaving the safety of the shore.

Other rescue services such as Police and Paramedics are all professionals in their own sphere and when necessary perform an invaluable assistance, but may not have the specialist equipment needed – for instance in a quicksands rescue. A life could be lost in a short time by asking for the wrong services.

No longer does the siren sound from the Grange bathing pool to warn of the incoming tide as the pool has been derelict for years, but a siren is operated manually from Arnside, and as the river now favours that side of the bay lots of holiday-makers paddle and tread for flukes during the summer and walk out on the sands from the caravan sites. This siren helps to make them aware of the

The rescue services – and especially Barrow's lifeboat – play a key role in the affairs of Morecambe Bay. (Top, left) The lifeboat crew;
(top, right) The old lifeboat station on Roa Island, seen in stormy conditions; (lower) The new station nears completion. (Alec Moore – 3).

dangerous incoming tide and warns them to leave the sand for the safety of the shore. This siren can also be heard from the Grange side of the estuary but only when the wind is in the right direction.

Morecambe Bay is renowned for its changing scenery and spectacular sunsets, but at high tides the bay is filled with such force and speed, taking away and depositing literally hundreds of tons of sand with each tide. Terms used by myself and other fishermen to describe these movements vary but are usually called "reigns". Sometimes these can be areas the extent of a football pitch. New sand moved in and deposited on one fast flow of tidal water meets up with another. The stronger flow stops the other in its tracks. On these fast tides the sand area is smooth and flat as a table top.

There is a prominent dividing line and towards that line the sand is more likely to be sugary and unstable, not a quicksand, but it would not allow man or machine, or even a group of walkers, to linger in that area. Once the tides drop down in height to the neaps (the low tides) these areas seem to harden.

The tide runs into the bay at a much faster rate than when it goes out. The flow of the river moves the sand more than at the ebb – the flow scours and does more damage, whereas the ebb deposits. Where ever the river bed lies, that is the lowest part of the bay.

With the river Kent being so far away from the Grange side I concentrate on looking towards the village of Silverdale at a high tide. Depending on favourable conditions and no wind, I can make out the white wall of water – the tidal bore – at approximately two hours before high tide. This force of water takes only two hours to fill the bay up to high water mark. However, it takes at least seven hours for the tide to ebb out to the same level....

~ THE GUIDE OVER THE SANDS ~

Now Cedric is the man we trust
To guide us o'er the sands
He knows the safest ways of all
Our lives are in his hands

Sometimes our path is dangerous
Where quicksands treacherous lie,
And when the river must be crossed,
With waters rushing by.

But there are places firm to tread,
Where hard sand is secure,
Here Cedric leads us skilfully
To the safety of the shore.

The journey of our life compares
With the crossing of the sands
We meet with many hazards
And are glad of helping hands.

For quicksands are around us
And high tides threat to flood
Across our paths of happiness
When going should be good.

But there's a Guide to help us
And lead us to firm sand,
Until we reach the other shore
And find the Promised Land.

Eileen M. Child.

THE FAMOUS MORECAMBE BAY WALK

Arnside, the seaside resort of Cumbria, is the people's choice as a starting point for the internationally known popular walk across Morecambe Bay. It has been described as one of the world's most wonderful journeys and you need not be an athlete to take part.

The bay covers about 120 square miles of sea and sandbanks and two main rivers – the Kent and the Leven, but at low tide, given good weather, this can dry out and appear desert-like – an English Sahara.

The route starts from the end of the promenade at Arnside and meanders for approximately eight miles with the river Kent crossing, which is always the highlight of this walk, and finishing up at Kents Bank railway station.

Every summer thousands of intrepid trippers put their trust in the Guide to take them safely across the bay. Then how do all these people arrive in order to make this fantastic journey?. Well, if you decide to come by car there is an alternative – either drive to Arnside arriving in good time to find a suitable parking place or as many people do, drive to Kents Bank railway station and park your vehicle and take the train to Arnside on the short but picturesque ride of about seven minutes as it rattles over the railway viaduct into Arnside railway station.

The walkers have congregated on the promenade opposite the Albion Hotel, the start of the walk each season for a number of years, but now with the build up of walkers and traffic through the village, for safety reasons we are obliged to start out from the end of the promenade. Not all those who have booked to come on the sands walk travel to the area by car.

Many, many different organisations from all parts of the country have booked well in advance of the start of the season's programme and these come to the village by coach usually. The passengers are dropped off near to the post office and parade of shops and the coach drivers then drives around the bay to Grange-over-Sands or Kents Bank where they await the walkers approximately three to three and a half hours later. No double deckers please as they cannot reach the village owing to a low railway bridge about half a mile short of the destination at Arnside!!

Before making out into the bay following a long bus ride almost everyone goes looking for the toilets. The ones at Arnside were not built to accommodate scores of people at one time, so there are usually queues. I remember getting on the train at Kents Bank station last season with quite a crowd of people who were coming on the sands walk.

We were crushed together like sardines in a tin so it was virtually impossible for the fares to be taken and we all got a free ride. Four women made themselves known to me and were really looking forward to the experience of crossing Morecambe bay, but they also told me that their husbands had crossed the sands the year previously and their advice to their wives was – once you meet up with Mr Robinson, do not leave his side whatever. I needed the toilets and made a beeline for them after walking the short distance from the railway station, but all four of these good ladies followed me in until they realised their mistake and made a quick exit!!

If the weather stays settled, this makes things much easier for me out on the sands, testing and marking out the route for the following days for the hundreds of walkers to cross safely.

Inclement weather can change the river and the sands dramatically in such a short time, so I am always very pleased when conditions are favourable. So many people seem to get so much out of the sands walks as you can imagine. When you leave the safety of the shore you have to put all your trust in your leader.

There are lots of watery areas to be crossed from time to time and sometimes quicksands to be avoided and then the river Kent has to be crossed and this is definitely the highlight of this unique walk. The depth can vary from around knee deep usually to up to the thigh, but during mid-season the sea-water temperature can be like that of warm water from the bathroom tap. Everyone loves this experience and halfway across the bay coming on to a much higher level, stopping for a break gives the walkers time to take in something quite different. – Almost like being in the middle of nowhere, away from the race of road traffic and its fumes. Peace and tranquility, with beauty all around.

For many of these worthy people a once in a lifetime experience. For many, throughout the season, have found satisfaction in doing something which they have really enjoyed and at the same time have raised many thousands of pounds for the charities of their choice.

One family, mam, dad and two young girls had enjoyed the experience of joining me on one of the walks which started from Arnside and they had previously done the lovely walk over Arnside Knott, the hill which gives them panoramic views across the estuary, the railway and the viaduct.

Their young children had never been on a train ride before, so to please them the family set out on their journey by road from Clitheroe to Arnside, arriving early before 9a.m. There were very few people around, so they parked their vehicle, a Volvo, on the car park near to the railway station where they had parked on previous visits.

They did not know that this particular day there was to be a high tide, with several feet of water covering the whole of the car park, so they left for the railway station and caught the train up to Whitehaven. This train ride follows the west coast shoreline for miles, so this was going to be so exciting for the children.

On the return train journey, looking from the train window, one little girl said "Oh look, there's all water round our car daddy" . "No" was his reply, "it's the suns reflections on the wet sand. The girl was right! When they did eventually arrive at the car park and opened the car doors, sea water just poured out.

The local folks at Arnside said that the vehicle had been bobbing about on the tide and had not the car park been bounderied off with huge boulders, the Volvo would have been taken back with the tide and out to sea.

The amazing thing, as the owner told me, was that when he put the keys in the ignition, the engine started immediately and he was able to drive carefully all the way back to Clitheroe – but everytime they went uphill they could hear water draining to the back of the vehicle and running out onto the road.

Whatever people following behind made of this they will never know. This nasty experience did not put them off coming back to Arnside, but they were given my name and telephone number to ask about tide times so as to avoid coming on the weekend of high tides and prevent anything like that happening to them again.

Never, in the history of the sands, has Morecambe Bay become as popular as it is today.

Walkers of all ages, from all walks of life – the rich and famous and the really down to earth people who all get together, meet and make new friends on the day and share in this unique experience.

Whatever the weather on the day, people still genuinely enjoy the walk with a difference and I can see from the expression on their faces at the end of the eight mile trek that some of them are tired, but they always say how much they have enjoyed crossing the sands.

The same cannot be said for a group of young schoolchildren I had guided across the sands and as we approached the shore at Kents Bank I could see that some of them were a little weary from the experience.

One little lass came up to me and said "Mr Robinson,

I'll never ever cross that bay with you again as long as I live" and her little friend who could not have been more than seven or eight years old, came alongside me, put her hands on her hips like a real madame and said "Well, after crossing these sands today with you Mr Robinson I think I can honestly say I can tackle anything".

Although one of many, this particular walk with these children left me with memories which I shall keep with me forever.

As we made our way from the sands and over the cobbly limestone ramp from the shore to the railway station, looking back at the huge expanse of sands I could see the tide in the distance moving in and the weather clouding over with a few spots of rain.

We had been lucky. The weather had kept fine for us until the end of the walk and I am sure that the topic of conversation on the coach trip home would have been something quite out of the ordinary.

～ DAISY'S WALK ～

There is a place called Morecambe Bay, oh it's a lovely spot.
Lots of people go there, especially when it's hot.
Most just go to lie there, swim or play or talk,
But every now and then people go to walk.
The walk it is a special one, it goes across the bay
It's seven miles through shifting sand and usually takes a
    day.
Daisy decided to do it, "It'll be a challenge" she said.
George said "I'm not going, you need someone to look at
    your head".
Daisy set off doggedly and soon she'd left the shore
With lots of other walkers, the Guide was to the fore.
The sand was hard and hurt the feet and then she hit the
    sea.
The day was fine but the water cold and Daisy cried
    "Dearie me".
As deeper they went , the Guide cried out "Don't worry
    I'll take care of you"
But Daisy was cold her only thought was "Blimey my
    nose has turned blue"
The water got deeper the further they went and soon it
    was over the knee.

Daisy thought "Well when it gets to me bum at least I
    can stop for a p..
No one will know just what's going on, this surely is the
    best place…
It'll warm me legs and no one will know if I keep the
    smile from me face"
So on and on dear Daisy went and achieved her final
    goal.
She thought as she took the few last steps "I could
    murder some tea and a roll".
Her skin was turning purple, she was as cold as can be.
A man took pity, "You're perished love, here have a drink
    of this tea".
Daisy sipped it gratefully then rang George to come in
    his van,
This he did because you know our George is a
    gentleman.
So Daisy this poem is coming your way to tell you how
    proud we all are,
You did it – you walked the whole seven miles –
Daisy you are a real star.

Jean Burdin-Sellers.

THE BALLAD OF MORECAMBE BAY
By T. R. TAYLOR
Commemorating an incident during the crossing of 16/6/1979.

Now Tha's heard of young Albert Ramsbottom,
    And Wallace, the Lion as well ?
And his stick with the 'orse's 'ead 'andle
    The finest that Woolworths could sell ?

But pin back thi lug oils a minit,
    Or, as Shakespeare would put it, perpend,
And I'll tell thee a more stirring story
    That'll mak thi 'air stand up on end.

The weather were quite unpropitious,
    As two coaches, at nine of the clock,
Drawn up near t'old Tech in Blackburn,
    Were beseiged by a right motley flock.

Now some were quite new to such ventures,
    And blissfully made quirks and quips,
They thought that Technician's bus outings,
    Were rather like Mr. Cook's trips!

But many, the seasoned campaigners,
    (Who'd been on excursions before,
From Galloways Mull to t'Malverns,
    They'd tramped with our Fred to the fore).

Knew better; Said one, "He has led us,
    For twentyfive years, pretty near,
Through rain, sleet, snow, slush, mud and peat bogs,
    And stuff quite unprintable here.

Across t'sands from Hest Bank we've plodded,
    Ten times, give or take once or twice,
We lost only four on t'last crossing.
    Well, three and a half, (kids half price).

The clouds now are gathering to Northwards,
    The Kent will be black as the slips,
But first comes the Keer, which, though smaller,
    Will probably drown about six.

Then we'll have to watch out for t'quicksands,
    I reckon, going on at this rate,
It's quite on t'cards that, this evening,
    One bus will hold all of us,mate"!

But these gloomy prognostications,
    Were lost in the clapping of hands,
For Fred, with his calm reassurance,
    To get them to Grange-over-Sands.

At last the bus loads were both settled,
    And carefully checked on Fred's list,
(You need to know who's there to start with,
    Or those lost on 't trip wouldn't be missed).

The coaches got safely to Heysham,
    And there made the Churchyard first call,
Where the party inspected stone coffins,
    (Who knew what might later befall).

Hest Bank was t'next destination,
  Where those who the weather defied
Set off walking the sands. Said non-walkers,
  "See you - (if you reach t'other side!)"

But prior to starting t'excursion,
  Their leader spoke up loud and clear;
"There's quicksands about for t'unwary,
  So howd on and give us thi ear.

Tha must not diverge from main party,
  What ? Cairns ? - we dont run to such frills,
Nor can tha look up t'route in Wainwright,
  He goes gallivantin on't hills.

Tha must follow t'guide without failure,
  and tread in his steps, heed me well,
Though, of course, if t'sands claim thee victim,
  Tha might get a plaque at Cartmel".

T'first stretch were perfectly easy,
  And some, in all innocence said,
"As long as we follow t'guides footprints,
  We'll all be as safe as our Fred".

But then came the Keer - a small river –
  Well, nobbut a beck at first glance,
But with t'bed notor-i-ously treach'rous,
  If churned up by folk in advance.

"If your not first across", Fred had told them,
  "Go steady, but don't stop to rest,
If tha feels the soft sand and mud sucking –
  Keep going- and hope for t'best".

So Fred took the hand of a youngster,
  Whose crossing this time were her first,
But, just for bad luck, in t'middle,
  He lit on a patch of t'worst.

As he slowly sank gradually deeper,
  He thought of occasions long past,
As a dying man's life is remembered,
  In the seconds he thinks are his last.

He thought of his trips from the College,
  Of weather, both foul and fine,
Of blizzards on t'Howgills in Springtime,
  And of Malham Cove bathed in sunshine.

Of wind blowing water up t'Downfall,
  Of floods on the Wharfe and t'Dalesway
Of snow in the gullies on Hopegill,
  And mist over Gable one day,.

" Of a tale that a dog bit Dick K.
  Noy likely" said Tom, "He's too slick.
A dog bitten him ? I'd lay money,
  The dog has been bitten by Dick ! "

He thought of his wife and his children,
  To be widowed, and orphaned that day,
It were first time he'd been drowned in t'quicksands,
  And he wondered what Mabel would say.

But just as a tear dimmed his eyesight,
  He felt firmer ground underneath,
Then willing help came from his colleagues;
  (Who'd been weighing up cost of a wreath !)

A Stalwart on each side said;"Easy,
  Hang on and we'll soon have thee free;
Tha'll arise from the waves like a Phoenix;
  Aphrodite had nothing on thee !"

But sadly to say, in misjudgement,
  They gave Fred a Concerted yank,
And, instead of his rising from t'seabed,
  The other two gradually sank !

T'weren't bad for one chap - a six footer
    But t'other, much shorter tha knows.
Went clean out of sight, but said Lofty,
    "S'all right, I've got hold of his clothes."

As the water lapped up round their shoulders,
    Said Lofty,"we'll be catching chills",
Said Fred, "What of Tich whose down under,
    Dost think he'll grow himself gills ?"

But their plight had been noticed by Dilys,
    Who, by then, was about on the verge,
Of calling their friends to attention,
    With t'idea of singing a dirge.

Sensing hope, she now sprang into action,
    And called across sands for t'guide,
By good luck he'd brought with him his tractor
    Since mayhap some kids might want a ride.

He soon got a rope round the duo,
    Who said, "Save us from watery graves",
But Tich of course, just gave a gurgle,
    He was holding his breath 'neath the waves !

The tractor began pulling slowly;
    The cheering crowd, duly impressed,
Saw Fred and Owd Lofty extracted,
    With Tich hauled along by his vest

Rather wet but no worse for their mishap,
    Were the three; nearly lost without trace,
(Though, with holding his breath for ten minutes,
    Tich was a bit red in't face).

Midst the cheers and congratulations,
    Of his friends, Fred returned to the van,
He led 'em through t'Kent, striding firmly,
    As though quicksands had been part of his plan.

"It were nothing," he said over shandy,
    In t'bar when they'd all got ashore,
"Come with us next year; if you wish it,
    I might even give an encore !".

Sent to me by Mr. Fred Gemmel, a retired Teacher from Blackburn Technical College. He crossed the Bay for many years until recently, when Anno Domini held him back !

ADVENTURES WITH THE SAND PILOT

The now famous walk currently starts from Arnside and ends up at Kents Bank railway station but in previous years the starting place for the walk was from Hest Bank foreshore near to Morecambe. The route taken across the sands was via Priest Scar and this would take us approximately three hours, stopping for a short break on the sands about half way across the bay and in line with Jenny Brown's Point but well out in the bay.

I led this walk for 23 years and on the Grange side we had to vary the place to come ashore accordingly as the river Kent moved, and this was at the Grange-over-Sands railway station sometimes or opposite the old bathing pool and more rarely at the Cart Lane Crossing. Kents Bank railway station was not the most convenient place to finish a walk in those earlier years.

With the river Kent running nearer to the Grange side of the bay, the organised walks could leave Hest Bank earlier on the tide, cross the river and land on the shore at Grange, have a short break and then do the return journey. I have done that often in the earlier days and on most occasions had the good company of Jim Lowther from Preston with his old pal, the late Gordon Handslip of Grange. Jim still does the Morecambe Bay walk.

One memorable crossing was from Hest Bank to Grange and then return. I had my tractor parked on the farmyard near to the shore at Bolton-le-Sands as I was putting fishing nets for plaice out in the bay towards the stone jetty at Morecambe.

This particular day, as it was school holidays, I took along my son Paul and daughter Jean and we went out and fished the nets and returned to Hest Bank shore to meet up with a group of walkers. Paul now took over the driving of the tractor with Jean sitting on the back with the fish. I led the walkers and away we went on our sands trek to Grange.

On leaving the group safely at the shore near to the Bathing Pool, I now took over the wheel of the tractor and we sped off back over the sands towards Hest Bank, following the same route. Once we had crossed the river Keer and now looking towards Morecambe and the stone jetty I noticed something out on the sands which was not there when we crossed with the walkers. As we came nearer I could see it was a Ford Escort van and a brand new one at that!

At low tide the sands at Hest Bank, Bolton-le-Sands can dry out looking relatively safe and inviting. People used to, and still do I suppose, drive vehicles out there learning to drive etc. but it is never advisable to leave the safety of the shore.

Seemingly, on this day two teenage lads employed on the building of the new M6 motorway decided to drive down to the shore for their lunch break. Adventurous, they travelled out to where the sand was less dry and rather soft near to a dyke and the vehicle was stuck down as far as the sills. What a lucky chance I turned up when I did on that day or those lads would have certainly lost this vehicle, not to mention their jobs. They were so pleased to see me at the shore with the van in tow as they had been in touch with the police who told them there was nothing they could do.

No policeman ever ventures out onto the sands without being accompanied by someone with knowledge and experience of the area – and who can blame them?

There are so many memories of those earlier walks; for instance, when a man with a wooden leg, a very determined person, joined us on one of the walks but he

A lifetime of achievement.
(Above) A much younger Cedric and his wife Olive on one of the early cross-Bay walks about 1964.
(Opposite) Cedric and Olive at Buckingham Palace in December 1999 after he had received the MBE
— an event described on pages 94 and 95. (Charles Green Photography)

had to abandon his attempt half way across at Jenny Brown's point as his wooden leg kept getting stuck in the softer sand and holding up everybody else. We made our way to the row of cottages at Jenny Brown's Point near Silverdale and made sure that he was alright and a taxi was ordered to take him back home. I suppose he felt terribly disappointed but it was for the best as 'time and tide waits for no man'.

A 92 year old man joined one of the walks and he had the company of his son to keep an eye on him. He accomplished the walk and said that he had enjoyed the experience very much and wondered if he was the oldest person ever to cross the sands. He was as far as I could remember and it was certainly a credit to him at his age and a great achievement.

A most memorable occasion was the doggy walk to raise money for the Dogs for the Blind. There must have been at least 200 dogs and their owners. What a wonderful day out for this group – with a difference. On our approach to the river the safe route to cross was marked with two laurel bushes on this side and two on the opposite side, giving a safe width to keep between. On this lovely day, dogs of all breeds, colours, shapes and sizes made a beeline for the first laurel bush, one after another, cocking their legs up alongside the first laurel and having a wee. They seemed to think that I had put the laurels there especially for this purpose and it was so amusing to watch them.

Anyone coming into Grange-over-Sands now and taking a walk along the promenade, looking out into the bay would never in a million years imagine that the river Kent at one time ran quite close to the shore at Grange and Kents Bank, but it did.

As a lad on leaving school my memories are of about 15 – 20 fishermen from Flookburgh including myself with horses and carts plus several Morecambe Trawler boats all in the river trawling for shrimps. Starting near Holme Island and going as far as Humphrey Head we had our boxes full of good quality shrimps and then we were homeward bound.

I believe the river stayed close to the Grange side for about 35 years and it was very deep. A rocky coastline can hold a river for a very long time. High tides, strong winds and heavy rainfall contribute to river changes and meandering but something quite dramatic happened out there in the bay when the Kent moved overnight for a distance of about four miles. Not in the memory of any living person had this happened before!

Although I had led the walks from Hest Bank, near Morecambe fo 23 years, it was now virtually impossible to follow that route, so a safe alternative was found by starting the walks from Silverdale for about four years and latterly from the village of Arnside.

Whereas previously on some of the walks many of the people did the return journey as this was just possible with a close margin of tide in the river Keer there could be no lingering, we just had to get a move on. As already mentioned though the walkers were few in number in those earlier days.

I had never heard of the cross-bay walks personally and I only lived a few miles away. Very rarely did one see children on the walk with their parents. Although the dates fixed for these walks were advertised iin the local press, they were still relatively unknown to outsiders and those who did take part on the walk seemed to be of a similar age group.

It is totally different today.

Walking the sands is now a national pastime with up to 30 or more walks per season from May to September and there are about 10,000 people of all ages sharing this same experience in the season.

I study the tides and choose the dates for these crossings in early January but my wife Olive takes the bookings and is currently overwhelmed by the demand which is usually on the telephone. A good percentage of these walks are now organised for almost every known charity and as already commented we have raised thousands of pounds as well as opening up a whole new world for the visitors.

A walk does not just happen!

Lots of time out on the sands is needed on the day prior to every crossing including checking the river and the route for the quicksands which have to be avoided. The river hardly ever stays in the the same place and moves with every tide so I have to go out there to make sure that on the following day the walkers will have a safe and enjoyable walk across the bay and nothing is left to chance. These days I usually have the company of my nephew Kenny and Mike, a good friend, as they both enjoy going out there and it makes it much easier for me especially on the days when we find the river difficult and it has taken us longer than expected to choose the safest possible route.

Every summer thousands of intrepid walkers put their trust in me to guide them safely across the bay so lots of preparation and time has to be spent, marking the route with laurel bushes which makes the trip for them a safe, unique and wonderful experience.

Its taken me a lifetime getting to know the bay in all its variable moods and they can be very variable. If it were to be the same every day I do not think that I would still be the Guide. One never knows what one will find out there and if the bay can catch you out, it certainly will, with a vengeance. The Guide has to go out to check the river and whatever the situation is, make the best of it. Things do not always turn out as planned but in all my 37 years of guiding, I can count on one hand how many times I have had to cancel a walk although it must be understood by organisers of groups, all persons, families or individuals wishing to take part in the sand walks that owing to foul weather which may render the crossing hazardous just prior to a walk or on the actual day the Guide may have to, at his discretion, cancel a walk. It is for their own safety that people ring prior to a walk rather than just turn up to be disappointed.

Yes, with all its moods, Morecambe Bay is still a magical place and that is why I can appreciate so many people want to return again and again to thoroughly enjoy this unique experience of crossing the sands and making it one of the most popular walks in the North west.

This could not have been achieved by me without the help and dedication of my wife, Olive, who spends endless hours on the telephone throughout the season in reply to requests for the dates and times of the walks, train information and other details to enable visitors to arrive at the right time and place.

I did have a setback when in 1994 I had to undergo heart bypass surgery and my family, that is my beloved wife Olive, five grown up and nine grandchildren were not sure if I would pull through, but the Lord must have been on my side. Not only have I recovered, but now eat a healthy diet, feel fitter than ever before, leading a very busy life on and off the sands during the summer months.

We still keep a few animals, to date a pedigree fell pony called Chester and three bullocks which I have reared from calves, five goats and 35 hens which lay lovely large brown eggs. The animals are always quiet as they see me regularly and thrive on my tender loving care.

In all the years here at the farm we have always been glad to see the swallows arriving and building their nests in the outbuildings. They are seen normally about the 20th April when they rear their young and then leave later in the year, usually during late August or early September. Olive and I believe they bring us good luck. Marvellous little birds, as when they leave their birthplace behind they have to remember the landmarks and feeding areas if they are to return. Bad weather is the biggest killer of migrating swallows, so clear weather is what they need if they are to survive. It is said that a swallow can see 60 miles in any direction when they climb to a height of three miles. After spending two months in South Africa they return and these wonderful and amazing birds remember their local landmarks.

As I sit here writing in the late evening, I have just heard the croaking of our first toad or frog *i.e. 12th March.* They seem to come earlier each year now with the season getting milder, probably something to do with the 'global

warming'. Last year we must have had at least 25-30 of each species on our fish pond.

Wild geese, notably the greylag, and duck have taken a liking to this area. They can be seen during the day and heard at night spending every minute feeding on the lush grassy area on the foreshore out from Guide's Farm. They arrived on the shorter wintery days and I have counted up to 200 mixed greylag and canada geese. Last year we had about 120 and they stayed here till the 15th March, so it will not be very long before these birds will be taking to the air and moving on, northwards.

To the birdwatcher, from the Grange promenade the solitary redshank feeds near to the shoreline and the rare curlew hunts for worms. Wild duck can be heard dabbling in the softer areas of sands with the widgeon, drakes with chestnut heads and buff crowns. The whistling criies are unmistakeable. When the tide turns theses armies of waders settle on the sands and feed on.

As the day draws on and the sun is setting in this magical bay the birds fly on to rest.

If the tides are very low, these birds will still be out there in the bay at night.

Seldom alone for too long!
(Opposite) Cedric has the Bay to himself on a glorious day far out on the sands. (Alan Mirfield)
(Above) Leading a walk with several hundred participants – a common occurrence now that some
10,000 people make the crossing each year. (Philip Dunn)

THOSE WHO CROSS

Guide's Farm, where we live, is right on the edge of the shore behind the railway embankment between Grange-over-Sands and Kents Bank. This is a tenanted 700 year old cottage with approximately 10 acres of land and it is owned by the Duchy of Lancaster.

Traditionally the former guides as well as me worked the smallholding but looking at the history of some of these guides, they did not follow the sands as I have done from a very early age, to earn their living, but they relied on the few acres they had and did a bit of farming on a small scale.

It must have been very hard for them to manage many a time as their salary was only £15. per annum from the Duchy. That has not changed and my official salary has remained at £15 annually since my appointment as Guide.

Something that has changed dramatically is the workload and the popularity of the Morecambe bay walks as they are now used by leisure walkers, parents and families, organised groups, school parties etc. etc. in ever increasing numbers. Many of these groups are dedicated to raising large sums of money for various charities year after year and in even larger numbers of walkers.

Last year, 1999, in the season from May to September no fewer than 10,000 people crossed the Morecambe Bay sands under my guidance. It has been estimated that over one-third of a million people have crossed the sands since my appointment.

They come from all countries and all walks of life, many of them being famous people.

One of my earliest experiences out in the bay was being filmed with the historian, A. J. P. Taylor. We were filmed near to Humphrey Head point and at one stage Professor Taylor managed to lag behind. Seemingly the sand had softened up a little with the weight of the group ahead of him and he, being the last, had panicked and stopped. I went back to him and jokingly asked him if he needed a piggy back. 'YES' he answered and needed no persuasion – he jumped on my back and I carried him on to an area of terrafirma and then dropped him. No doubt I was the only person to give a piggy back ride to this famous person in Morecambe bay!

A few weeks later I was being filmed for a children's T.V. programme and on our return I heard that two families – eight people in all – had been trapped in quicksands for up to an hour and a quarter near Heversham. That is in the upper reaches of the Kent estuary above the Arnside railway viaduct.

The two families managed to free themselves with the help of local farmers and a resident who also went to their assistance. Three members of the party were taken to the Wetmorland County Hospital where they were treated for shock and exposure.

They had been walking along the sands off Marsh Lane with some close friends about 100 yards off the shore when this happened. Within seconds all eight of them found themselves trapped up to their knees in quicksand. After a struggle the children managed to crawl out to safety, but their parents, weighed down with wellingtons and thick jumpers just sunk deeper. Mrs Bolton sank up to her chest and two men were up to their waists – a really terrifying experience. The T.V. producer who was with me at the time when we heard what had happened thought 'if I could only get this on camera and interview them, it would be great' but they declined the offer of this publicity as their ordeal had been so frightening they did not want reminding of it. They just wanted to forget the whole experience.

Sands are tempting when they dry out at low tide and in fine weather. They seem to draw people out there rather like a magnet. DO NOT be fooled by this as danger is always there for the unwary. NEVER attempt to walk on to the sands unless accompanied by someone with local knowledge of them as to know them you have to live with them.

Bob Langley, a well known TV personality and writer who has done many outdoors programmes, met me at the farm and was later filmed in the bay for a film which was called 'Lakeland Summer'.

Magnus Pike, a professor and certainly a great personality who 'spoke with his arms', never still but an extremely clever chap. Morecambe bay again on T.V. with a programme called 'Don't Ask Me' when an audience would ask questions at random. This particular question was 'What makes quicksands'. The filming was done close to the shore, out from Guide's farm with extremely dangerous quicksands in which one person and a huge air/sea rescue helicopter were involved. Quite frightening but amusing at the same time.

Judith Chalmers from T.V. holiday programme 'Wish you were here'. Judith loved the area and being filmed in the bay crossing the river.

The Blue Peter programme filmed in the bay and as we all know, as the years go by, many of these programmes seem to get new and younger presenters appearing on our screens. At the time of filming out there, a nice, pleasant young chap by the name of Simon Groom was accompanied by the famous Blue Peter dog, Goldie.

I enjoyed every minute of being out there and the filming of these programmes.

Matthew Kelly, who is now well established on television , and I must say that the tide has been in and out of Morecambe Bay many times since first meeting him at Kents Bank station with his film crew when I was introduced to him. He said to me "You're quite famous Cedric, aren't you? You've been on T.V. more than I have". I probably had been at that time, but he was a humorous kind of chap and after the filming on the sands this group including my wife Olive and myself were all invited to have tea at Abbot Hall, Kents Bank where Mr David Mycock was the manager. We have some brilliant photographs of this event in colour which bring back happy memories.

In 1985 I had an enquiry from the London office of Melvyn Bragg asking 'Would it be possible to accompany him across the sands of Morecambe Bay?' Yes, I agreed to take him in early May. It was a lovely day with sunshine for us. My daughter Jean drove me round to the other side of the bay to meet him on the shore near Hest Bank. It took Melvyn and I over four hours to cross. Seemingly this journey was for him to get the feeling of the sands crossing into his mind and his blood so this would be a genuine contribution to a book he was writing called ' The Maid of Buttermere'.

David Bellamy, now a professor, came to see us at the farm and eventually we went on the sands at Kents Bank to take a film with a group of schoolchildren on a lovely sunny day out cockle fishing and at the fluke nets. On the way home we were all singing the song 'Cockles and mussels alive, alive ho' and I have got a video of that lovely little film to prove it!

Ray Gosling came to see us on more than one occasion and again we filmed out on the bay.

Russell Harty visited us and that was a day to remember as it poured with rain the whole of the time. Poor old Russell spoke to me out on the sands and said "Cedric, a man could die out here and nobody would know". He did die later, but not on the sands.

Bob Grundy – do you remember him? Many people will. He was also a visitor to Guide's Farm.

Treasure Hunt with Annabelle Croft was a wonderful experience with the horses and carriages belonging to Mr George Bowman of Penrith taking part. I did not think

(Top) School children dash to the shore.
(Left) A cross-Bay carriage drive returning
to Kent's Bank, with Cedric in the leading
carriage. (Fred Broomfield — 2)

(Top) The writer Jessie Anderson (left) with grand-daughter Sarah Victoria Robley (centre) and Sarah Haliburton during a crossing in 1999. (Jonathan Becker)
(Lower) Hannah Hauxwell signing a copy of her book for Olive at Guide's Farm. (Fred Broomfield)

that the helicopter was ever going to spot us.

It was a most wonderful experience meeting up with Sir Harry Secombe, to be filmed for the Sunday programme 'Highway'. Once again we met at Kents Bank railway station to be filmed out on the bay on what turned out to be very, very blustery weather.

The American author Bill Bryson enjoyed his trip across the sands with a group of local people under my guidance. A lovely memorable day with Bill saying that the river Kent was the only river he knew which is under water most of the time. Quite true!

I was asked to accompany a group of very nice people out onto the sands via tractor and sandpiper. This event took place last summer on a beautiful sunny day. The group called themselves 'The Gaskell Society' and all of them were historians and were interested in the life and times of the writer Elizabeth Gaskell. This was later shown on the television programme 'Omnibus' and it came over very well.

A well-known Lakeland author and writer of guide books to the lakes is Hunter Davies. Hunter, accompanied by his wife, came on one of my bay walks and enjoyed it so much, he wrote a lovely article about their experience and later included it in a book he was compiling called 'From London to Loweswater'.

The list of famous people who have been to Guide's Farm and been taken onto these famous sands seems endless and still, as each new season comes along someone else will ring up right out of the blue with an enquiry.

A film documentary was made for French television showing the bay at its best including our methods of fishing – cockling, shrimping and fluke fishing. I think something good came from this filming as now all the cockles gathered in the bay by the Flookburgh fishermen, apart from the local orders, are sent over to France to be eaten raw, so they have to be despatched while they are still alive and fresh.

Barry Cockcroft who has now retired from television work but was a T.V. producer for Yorkshire television for many years became well known to our family. He made a documentary of the work of the Flookburgh fishermen for which I was spokesman and in later years I have still kept in touch with him. Barry was the person who discovered Hannah Hauxwell in the Dales on a lone farm and now Hannah loves to come to Grange-over-Sands to visit us and have a chat. She stayed with us last year for a week when I had a book published 'Sand Pilot of Morecambe Bay'. Hannah went with Olive and me round the book shops promoting my new book which we thought was very good of her.

Victoria Wood, the well known comedian and writer, who so often appears on T.V., crossed the sands. She was accompanied by a minder and kept herself disguised by wearing a hat with a large peak at the front held down low over her eyes so she would not be recognised!

Not so with Hayley from Coronation Street (Julie Hesmondhalgh). She joined in with everyone but it was a lousy day, weatherwise, for the walk. Afterwards everyone was invited back to Abbot Hall where we had sandwiches and tea or coffee. Hayley met everybody and had a good laugh. It had been a great experience for her to cross the bay and not only that but raised a lot of money for a very good cause, Parkinson's Disease to which people gave generously.

Yes, looking back over the years our lives have been very busy but so interesting.

Journalists too have always shown an interest in the bay with their own way of describing the adventure and nearly always providing superb pictures to illustrate the script.

The bay is such a wonderful place and a photographer's dream with such fantastic light and shade out there. This new experience of being somewhere special seems to inspire them and they just do not want it to end. A book of photographs called 'On Morecambe Bay' by Peter Cherry has the most sensational pictures one could ever imagine.

David Herrod, photographer from Cockermouth in Cumbria took some very unusual photographs of me on the sands and held an exhibition of them entitled 'Famous Cumbrian Folk' at the Barrow Maritime Museum and at Kendal Brewery Arts Centre to which Olive and I were invited for the preview.

Another special invitation was to the preview of photographs hung in the National Portraits Gallery in London. The photograph of me was by Julian Calder, taken out in the bay and used in a chapter headed 'The Ancient Offices of Britain' in a fabulous book entitled 'Keepers of the Kingdom' by Alastair Bruce. I understand that the first copy of this beautiful book was given to Her Majesty the Queen.

I do not think of myself as a writer but that of a simple fisherman and Queen's Guide to the sands. However, in my own style I have dabbled in writing now on a few occasions about something for which I have the love and respect – my beloved sands!

Over the years there have been several appearances on TV, radio interviews and I have had articles written about me in magazines and it has been gratifying to have taken part in all of these things. One thing I really do enjoy now however, is sharing these experiences with an audience. Many evenings during the wintertime Olive and I visit towns and villages where I am invited to speak about my work.

Being a member of H.M. Coastguard service means that one may be called upon day and night in an emergency. One such call several years ago was from the C.I.D. on Grange railway station promenade just after midnight. Olive and I had gone upstairs to bed about 11pm that night and we were asleep when the phone call woke us up. Seemingly, when the station porter was closing down the station after the last train of the day

which was nearly midnight, the lights from the station showed something which looked suspicious not far out from the promenade in the sands.

The police were gathered on the promenade when I arrived as they would not venture out on the sands in the dark, knowing the danger there. I was asked to go out towards this dark figure but not in a straight line as this would leave my footprints. I could see straight away that this was the body of a man lying face down and I could also see that his footprints from the shore were still visible in the mud as the tide had not taken them away. On my report I noted that six policemen followed me on to the sands with a stretcher in which we brought the body back to the shore. The body was that of an elderly resident of Grange who decided to end his life this way by walking into the tide. This incident took me a long time to get over, but it must have been a terrible shock for the relatives of this person, that is, if he had any.

Night visits to the sands are rare these days, but I still fish and set nets out in the bay to catch the tasty white flukes.

The Universities of Lancaster and Preston, central Lancashire both awarded me with honorary degrees of M.Sc. and made me an Honorary Fellow of the University of Central Lancashire.

The year of 1998 seemed to be a very good year – the Cumbria Tourist Board voted me 'Personality of the Year' and in 1999 I won the Barcleys Bank award in 'The Lakeland Book of the Year' for 'Sand Pilot of Morecambe Bay' which was unexpected but very pleasing.

In the Queen's birthday honours list in 1999 I was given the MBE – The Most Excellent Order of the British Empire and on the 2nd December 1999 attended the investiture at Buckingham Palace to receive my medal from Her Majesty the Queen.

Children – gloriously happy and covered in wet sand – find a trip out into the Bay a never-to-be-forgotten experience. The fish are (left) a fluke and a grey mullet. (Paul Nickson – 2)

Caton S.t. Pauls school
Brookhouse
Lancashire
LA2 9PJ
10th July 1998

Dear Mr Robinson,
    Thankyou for taking us out
on the sands it was brilliant, the
best school trip I've ever been
on. I wish there were more flat
fish then we could have taken
them home. The best bit was
the muddy puddles and the slip-
pery jellyfish, they slipped about
on your hands and went everywhere, I'm glad they weren't stingers.
Poor Alex that's the girl that got
stung but I think shes alright
now. Thankyou very, very, very,
very much.
                from
                Lauren Williams.

Just one of the many thankyou letters that Cedric has received from children who have completed the walk.

THE SANDS OF MORECAMBE BAY

Men, women and children line the shore at Arnside,
Ready to follow Cedric, the local sand guide.
For in the name of charity, on this August day,
We're venturing across the sands of Morecambe Bay.

By car, coach and mini-bus they've travelled in,
On the train they didn't pay – what a sin!
Five hundred and fifty people now gather round,
Collecting their stickers and paying their pound.

Ced blows his whistle and we follow in style,
Making the largest ever human crocodile.
Mums, Dads and children, and babies on backs,
All equipped with food, drinks and anoraks.

Keeping close to the shore, we follow round,
Passing through farm and caravan compound.
At Silverdale we pause for a while,
And unite again, our straggling crocodile.

We move in block across the sands,
Behind our guide – some holding hands.
The sun is warm, the sky is clear,
To the river crossing we are drawing near.

The footwear worn is quite varied indeed,
Of shoes and socks some feel they have no need.
Wellies, boots and trainers, all march along in line,
With Winfield's special offers at two pounds ninety-nine.

Ced blows his whistle when we reach the water's edge,
A long line he makes us form, instead of a big wedge.
Splish, splash, splish, splash – now we're getting wet,
On moving straight ahead, our intentions are set.

Alsatian, Terrier, Poodle and German Dachshund,
All start to swim now, as their feet have left the ground.
Jack Russell, Spaniel, Doberman and Heinz 57,
Enjoying every moment of this seventh heaven.

We reach the other side, with shrieks of fun and laughter,
Not caring how wet we are, we'll soon dry out after.
We pause again and some have lunch,
Bags of crisps, sweets or apples munch.

We are off again, but veer to the right,
Kent's Bank station now looms in sight.
The bristling wind reaches its highest peak,
We battle on, our journey's end we seek.

'Whose bright idea was this?' we keep asking,
As waterproofs rustle and legs are tiring.
The wind is so strong we have to tack,
And children hitch a lift by piggy back.

Kent's Bank station is now in full view,
Friends are waiting to greet us anew.
The van is there to sell ice cream,
As we wade through the final stream.

We collect our proof of completed mission,
Then attend a photographic session.
King George's Sailors have done well today,
From five hundred and fifty crossing Morecambe Bay.

Pauline M. Hutchinson (12th August, 1989)

OPEN TO ALL TRAFFIC?

On the 2nd September 1992, I received a letter from a Mrs Hartley, Clerk to the Council, Slyne with Hest Bank Parish Council and agreed with the sentiments of the council in objecting in the strongest possible terms to the Order dated 14th July l992 submitted by the Lancashire County Council to te effect that the route across the sands of Morecambe Bay from the shore at Hest Bank to the Lancashire/Cumbrian Boundary shown on the definitive maps of Public Rights of Way as a continuous line of roads used mainly as public paths (R.U.P.Ps.) be redefined as a Byeway open to all Vehicular Traffic (in accordance with the Wildlife and Countryside Act 1981).

In referring to Lancashire County Council's letter dated 7th August 1992, their reply was that 'they were dismayed that the Public Rights of Way subcommittees should recommend re-classification as a Byeway without agreeing firm proposals in respect of the safety of individuals who may attempt to cross the sands without the assistance of the Guide'.

Safety is of prime concern and the tragic loss of a single individual in attempting the crossing would result in a public outcry.

I was first made aware of this reclassification order when I received a phone call from the Lancashire County Council offices at Preston.

After a comprehensive explanation a date was fixed for someone from the Council to meet up with me at Guide's Farm. The day was warm and sunny when they arrived so the interview with me was outside as three of us sat on seats on the lane and looked out across the bay. My opinion and views were expressed and a recording which lasted well over an hour was taken.

At thiis early stage they listened and after the recording they seemed to agree with what I had to say.

A second and much longer and detailed interview took place again at the farm with different people including a Solicitor of the Council.

My personal objections to the proposal, additional to those raised by the Parish Council were as follows:-

1. The route would always require the expertise of an experienced guide because – it is not always possible to make a crossing due to high tides and severe weather conditions and quicksands. Timing of high tides and knowledge of incoming tides is critical. The exact route of a crossing can vary from day to day, again affected by tides, storms etc. in order to avoid quicksands and deep channels.

2. Even in extremely favourable conditions the crossing would have to be restricted to certain types of vehicular traffic. The reclassification as a byeway implies that any vehicle could attempt the crossing.

3. With reference to the Map Enclosure submitted with theLancashire County Council letter the route outlined for the crossing of the bay is currently impossible due to changes in the location of the Kent channel

4. Recent examples of problems affecting individuals on the sands:- The danger of vehicular traffic from my experience of rescue is that once the vehicle becomes stuck out there in quicksands the owners always seem reluctant to leave the vehicle, thus putting their lives in danger as well as their vehicle. Luckily we have an efficient coastguard service and most mishaps are reported in time to operate a rescue, but sadly, people still lose their lives out there, either through being stuck in the dreaded quicksands or cut off by the tide.

Storm and sunshine.
(Left) Morecambe Bay at its most
dramatic with a spectacular display of
lightning over Arnside Knott.
(Kenny Hopper)
(Right) Silvery sands and sun-flecked
water as far as the eye can see.
(Jonathan Becker)

Issues of safety, although taken very seriously by the County Council could not be considered when reclassifying an RUPP.

The only evidence which could have been considered was that which related to public rights along the route.

However, for the benefit of the general public a warning sign was erected by Cumbria County Council on the foreshore at Kents Bank and a similar one erected by Lancashire County Council on the Lancashire shore at Hest Bank.

The sign reads "Warning - the right of way across the bay to Kents Bank crosses dangerous sands. Do not attempt to cross without the official Guide". It then gives my name and telephone number.

Following the reclassification and the publicity two families on separate occasions attempted to cross the bay in their vehicles (4x4s) and got bogged down. One managed to get free but the other one is still out there with just the roof showing as a reminder of what can happen. Luckily the passengers were saved.

My recommendations are as follows:-

The Wildlife and Countryside Act of 1981 be amended to take into account the specific needs appertaining to the crossing of Tidal Waterways.

Public rights of way across Morecambe Bay to be permitted ONLY with the assistance of the officially appointed guide for reasons of safety.

BIRDS OF MORECAMBE BAY

Morecambe Bay, famed for it's breathtaking sunsets, is a home for most of the year to one of the largest concentrations of birds to be found anywhere in Europe.

Tens of thousands of birds – wildfowl, gulls, terns, cormorants and many other groups are drawn by the abundance of ready available food and by the safe resting and nesting sites provided by the sheltered shores and islands of the bay.

The most striking feature of the bay is its size – 120 square miles of sand and mud are exposed at low water making it the largest intertidal area in Britain.

Seven rivers feed into the bay; the river Leven is the overspill from Lake Windermere and the Crake runs into the upper reaches of the estuary at Greenodd near Ulverston on the west side of the bay. The river Kent starts up the valley above Kentmere and then winds its way south through Staveley and Kendal and into the upper reaches of the bay at Sandside, where it is met with the Bela river and meanders from one side of the sandy reaches to the other finding its own course towards Arnside, then through the railway viaduct and out into the bay on the east side. The river Winster enters at Grange and the Keer enters the bay at Carnforth . The river Lune adds to these at the mouth of the bay.

The bay is the most important wintering site in the United Kingdom for dunlin and oyster catcher.

The dunlin being so small with quick movement on the sands when they are feeding are named by the fisherfolk, including myself, mice, and the oystercatcher with it's black and white plumage and orange bills are distinctive and, when grouped together, resemble little men in dinner jackets.

The lapwing also has black and white plumage and large flocks can be seen on the upper reaches of the estuaries and at times on the sandbanks and salt marshes. They breed on the saltmarshes and fields around the bay.

The curlew is a large wader recognised by its brown streaked plumage, long decurved bill and familiar whistling call. It is a very wary bird and takes to the wing at the first sign of danger.

The redshank has a marly brown plumage, but with a white trailing edge to the wing. Its red legs are it's distinguishing feature.

The shellduck, quite a large duck, which stands out on the bay on a clear summer day, being generally white with a chestnut breast band and green head breeds in some numbers around the bay and it nests in rabbit holes. The young birds are brought down to the estuary as soon as they are hatched.

For the past two seasons my wife and I have witnessed this remarkable sight of mother, with up to 12 young ducklings coming down the middle of Carter Road and making for the shore. The only setback is that they have to cross the railway track safely to make it out onto the sands. As we watched they trundled onwards down the steep Carter Road and as we followed them at a distance in the car, we prayed to God that no other vehicle would come the other way and disperse them, but luckily they kept well together to the bottom of the hill, then turned right for Guide's Farm.

Olive and I left our car at the road end and walked slowly behind at quite a distance, watching the route they would take. Past Guide's Farm and through the stile on the footpath, and then they decided to cross the railway line now – another hazard - but all was clear and mother

Birds of Morecambe Bay as portrayed by the artist Fiona Clucas.
(Opposite) Sands at Sandside — with a curlew on the shore.
(Top) Paddling through reflected cloud — a study of lapwings.
(Right) Oyster catchers.

waddled down the grassy embankment and waited for her young, but not for long. As we watched them some managed to stay upright and others just rolled from the top to the bottom like small bundles of yellow and brown fluff, but did not seem any the worse. Then all set off together, crossed the railway line and made off on the other side through the brush and onto the foreshore. Quite remarkable!

Up to 1,000 of these birds can be seen at one time on the Kent estuary and the total wintering population can reach up to 7,500.

Pintail is easily recognised – the drake with its long tail combined with a striking pattern of brown head and throat with a white breast and stripe up the side of the neck. The duck has a more pointed tail and slender neck than other species.

Large numbers are seen on the bay, on Flookburgh marshes and on the Kent estuary. They are often seen on the tide at high water opposite Guide's Farm.

Amongst the gulls are the common gull, the lesser black-backed gull and the herring gull. The commonest of the three is the herring gull.

The cormorant is a large blackish water bird with white chin and cheeks. I usually see these out in the bay on the edge of the river. The shag is smaller and often stands with its wings held out. At high tide they often haul out onto the salt marshes or the trees on Chapel Island. When I was a young lad fishing with my father the cormorant had a price on it's head. It was thought that they were taking too many fish from the bay, so half-a-crown, old money, (now 25 pence) was paid to the fishermen for each head he gave to the fishery officer. We did not catch them – they caught themselves! As they dived down under the tide to take the fish from the fishery nets, they got themselves entangled in the meshing. When the tide turned and the nets began to show, you would always find one or two drowned cormorants, bring them home, chop off their heads and keep them until the fishery officer paid a visit to the area and he would pick up these and pay you your dues.

The birds of Morecambe Bay are now protected and I love to see, hear and watch them out there on what has been called "The Wet Sahara".

GUIDE'S FARM

The farm is situated on an east-facing slope overlooking Morecambe Bay. There are a number of valuable habitats on the farm but their interest is heightened by the fact that they are present over carboniferous limestone with a distinct maritime climatic influence, Grange having the highest spring temperatures in the North of England.

Habitats present on the farm include two hay meadows, two pastures, tall multi-species (and presumably old) hedges, limestone drystone walls and some small areas of scrub.

The farm is also of historic value since for many centuries it has been part of the remuneration for the King or Queen's Guide over the Sands – the post currently held by myself, Cedric Robinson, M.B.E.

There is one very busy footpath along the bottom of the meadows which gives passers-by an excellent view of them especially when they are in full flower in June and July. It is interesting to note that entrance to each end of the footpath has a special kind of gate which stops the animals getting out. They are known locally as kissing-gates.

The land is designated as an "important open area" in the South Lakeland District Council's local plan and is part of the Grange-over-Sands Conservation Area.

There is scope for the provision of some interpretation of the land, its historic associations and how it needs to be managed by traditional farming practices to maintain its wildlife and beauty. This is especially important since there is heavy use of the one public footpath by local people from the town and visitors alike, running along the coast as it does from Grange-over-Sands to Kents Bank. Whilst there is no pressure for developing the land for housing at the present time, the Countryside Stewardship Scheme and interpretation that it might grant aid, would also go a long way to enforcing the designation as a green area, but more importantly will help protect it as an important open area which is managed by traditional farming methods.

APPENDIX - Species List for Guide's Farm, Cart Lane, Grange-over-Sands 10th may 1998

Species are listed and their occurrence on different parts of the farm is noted as m = meadow p = pasture 1 = around limestone outcrops in pasture e = close to, or in the field boundaries

	Common Name	Scientific Name	m	p	l	e
1	sycamore	Acer pseudoplatanns				+
2	yarrow	Achillea millefolium	+	+		
3	bugle	Ajuga replans			+	
4	glabrous ladies mantle	Alchemilla glabra			+	
5	garlic mustard	Alliaria peliolata				+
6	wild garlic, or ramsons	Allium ursinum			+	+
7	sweet vernal grass	Anthoxanlhum odoratum	+	+		
8	cow parsley	Anthriscus sylvestris				+
9	parsley-piert	Aphanes arvensis			+	
10	lesser burdock	Arctium minus				+
11	cuckoo pint	Arum maculatum			+	+
12	daisy	Bellis perennis	+	+		
13	barberry	Berberis sp.				+
14	false brome	Brachypodium sylvaticum				+
15	soft brome	Bromus mollis	+			
16	hairy bittercress	Cardamine hisuta			+	+
17	lady's smock	Cardamine pratense	+	+		
18	spring sedge	Carex caryophyllea			+	
19	black knapweed	Centauria nigra	+	+		
20	field mouse-ear	Cerastium fontanum	+	+		
21	sticky mouse-ear	Cerastium glomeratum			+	+
22	little mouse-ear	Cerastium semidecandrum				+

(Top) One of the traditional hay meadows at Guide's Farm, noted for its rich flora. (Peter Cherry)
(Lower) Feeding goats at the farm prior to milking. (Fred Broomfield)

Common Name	Scientific Name	m	p	l	e	Common Name	Scientific Name	m	p	l	e
23 pignut	Conopodium majus	+	+			59 barren strawberry	Potentilla sterilis			+	+
24 hazel	Coryllus avellana				+	60 cowslip	Primula veris				+
25 hawthorn	Crataegus monogyna				+	61 self heal	Prunella vulgaris	+	+		
26 crosswort	Cruciata laevipes				+	62 blackthorn	Prunus spinosa				+
27 crested dog's tail	Cynosurus cristatus	+				63 meadow buttercup	Ranunculus acris	+	+		
28 cocksfoot	Dactylis glomerata	+				64 bulbous buttercup	Ranunculus bulbosus	+	+		
29 foxglove	Digitalis purpurea			+		65 lesser celandine	Ranunculusfrcaria	+	+		
30 male fern	Dryopteris filix-mas				+	66 creeping buttercup	Ranunculus repens	+	+		
31 bluebell	Endymion non-scriptus			+	+	67 buckthorn	Rhamnus cathartica				+
32 red fescue	Festuca rubra	+				68 yellow rattle	Rhinanthus minor	+			
33 wild strawberry	Fragaria vesca			+	+	69 wild gooseberry	Ribes uva-crispa				+
34 ash	Fraxinus excelsior				+	70 dog rose	Rosa canina				+
35 goosegrass	Galium aparine				+	71 blackberry	Rubusfruticosus agg.				+
36 herb robert	Geranium robertianum				+	72 common sorrel	Amer acehosa	+	+		
37 wood avens	Geum urbanum				+	73 curled dock	Rumex crispus				+
38 ground ivy	Glechoma hederacea				+	74 broadleaved dock (in gateways)	Rumex obtusifolius	+			
39 ivy	Hedera helix			+	+	75 elder	Sambucus nigra				+
40 hogweed	Heracleum sphondilium				+	76 salad burnet	Sanguisorba minor			+	
41 yorkshire fog	Holcus lanatus	+	+			77 ragwort(rare)	Senecio javobaea	+	+		
42 cat's-ear	Hypochaeris radicala	+				78 red campion	Silene dioica			+	+
43 holly	Ilex aquifohum			+		79 betony	Stachys of ficinalis			+	
44 meadow vetchling	Lathyrus pratense				+	80 hedge woundwort	Stachys sylvatica				+
45 rough hawkbit	Leontodon hispidus	+				81 greater stitchwort	Stellaria holostea				+
46 ox-eye daisy	Leucmhemum vulgare	+		+		82 black bryony	Tamus communis				+
47 perennial ryegrass (small amounts)	Lolium perenne	+				83 dandelion	Taraxacum sp.				+
48 birds foot trefoil	Lotus corniculatus				+	84 common lime	Tilia X vulgaris				+
49 field woodrush	Luzula campestris	+	+			85 lesser trefoil	Trifolium dubium	+			
50 dogs mercury	Mercurialis perennis			+	+	86 red clover	Trifolium pratense	+			
51 restharrow	Ononis repens			+		87 clover	7rifohum ;SP.		+		
52 wood sorrel	Oxalis acetosella			+		88 elm	Ulmus Sp.				+
53 meadow foxtail	Phleum pratense	+				89 nettle	Urtica dioica				+
54 hart'-tongue fern	Phyllitisscolopendrium				+	90 germander speedwell	Veronica chamaedrys			+	+
55 mouse-ear hawkweed	Pilosella officinarum			+		91 slender speedwell	Veronica filiformis	+			
56 ribwort plantain	Plantago lanceolata	+	+			92 thyme-leaved speedwell	Veronica serpyllifolia	+			
57 meadow grass	Poa pratense				+	93 bush vetch	Vicia sepium				+
58 tormentil	Potentilla erecta			+		94 dog violet	Viola riviniana			+	

DANGER! – QUICKSANDS

In the spring of 1999 I received a telepone call from New York – several in fact over a period of a few weeks. An American TV company had found my name through the internet and enquired whether it would be possible to come over to Heathrow, London, England and then travel up by hire car to Grange-over-Sands so that I could take them out into the Bay to film the quicksands.

I agreed over the telephone to take the film crew out after checking the tidetable and our very full diary. A date and time was fixed eventually to meet up with these guys with very strong American accents at Kents Bank Railway Station.

I had already prebooked a school party of thirty children for an educational walk out into th e Bay, but they assured me that this would not be a problem and agreed to combine the two events.

My own thoughts were that if they were willing to cross the Atlantic to make a film I must find them something worthwhile to film – something really, really dangerous!! So I set out into the Bay by tractor and made my way over towards Silverdale on the edge of the River Kent.

The quicksands at a glance were FRIGHTENING!. I always carry a long stick with me which I use to prod the sands in front of me as I tread with care.

My wife Olive is always concerned when I go out alone on these missions and she asks me to promise her that I do not take too many risks – Bless her. She will probably keep her eyes on me through the binoculars but this is not always possible when I am hidden from view at the lower level of the river.

As the tide comes tumbling in faster than a horse can gallop, it's ever changing and formidable quicksands are formed.

The sands change each day and the rivers are forever on the move. To the layman the sands look flat, but they are not and there can be variations of ten feet or more in places from the bed of the river to a higher sandbank.

There is a special vocabulary spoken by the fisherfolk – including me – out on the sands.

The large holes scoured out by the incoming tides are known as melgraves (i.e. deep holes) and on the ebb tide areas where the sand has formed and trapped water and air beneath the surface of these holes are the worst quicksands to be found and can set round a person, once in there, just like cement.

If ever you are unlucky enough to come into contact with quicksands, my advice would be to lie across with your arms outstretched and, by spreading your weight, this stops you sinking. The experts say that you are more buoyant in quicksands than you are in water, but do NOT be foolish enough to go out on the sands without someone with knowledge of the area, or you may just get more than you bargained for.

Quicksand is not as straightforward as water. A suspension of sand and water has one very peculiar behaviour. It freezes into a solid mass if you try to move through it rapidly.

Another major problem is that quicksands, unlike water, does not easily let go.

If you try to pull a limb out of quicksands, you have to work against a vacuum left behind, which is almost impossible, especially if you are out there alone. Luckily, we have a very efficient coastguard service stationed at Arnside with all the up-to-date eqipment for such incidents and there is hardly a season goes by without these services being called upon.

When the American film crew arrived and I met with them at Kents Bank Railway station, I was really surprised to see how young they were, and when I explained about the quicksands I had found for them to film, they thought of them as being too dangerous as they did not want to take any risks out there so far away from the safety of the shore, so I agreed to find them some slightly milder quicksands nearer to the shore in a dyke, a much smaller drain off than the River Kent and after looking this area over, it was just perfect for their requirements.

I was able to take hold of one of the small children's hand and walk over the quicksands area as long as we we kept on the move.

This was filmed and came over really well on television.

 Without taking too many risks, this was educational to all the children I took out onto the sands to be filmed for the National Geographical Documentary Programme.

Despite the danger, it still has to be said that even today the crossing of the sands of Morecambe Bay is more popular now than ever before in the history of the sands crossings.

The bay area is a tourist attraction, bringing thousands of visitors to the district during the summer season and many of these people at some time or other will venture out on to the sands.

Morecambe Bay is a notorious quicksand area which has claimed countless lives in the past. Each year my colleagues and good friends, the Arnside Coastguard Service carry out at least thirty quicksand rescues, mostly of holiday-makers who wander out and become trapped.

Finally – back to the film crew – when the film had been completed, I had a telephone call from New York informing me of the date fixed to be shown here in England on Sky Television. We do not have Sky TV so they offered to send us a video of the film. In the meantime my sister Jean had watched and recorded the programme and gave a copy to me.

It certainly was compulsive viewing – all the way through – gripping, starting with Morecambe Bay and finishing with shots of the bay.

Other quicksand areas around the world were filmed and even my colleagues at Arnside Coastguard Service and I were to learn something from the methods of rescue they used in other parts of the world, although very similar to what the Arnside lads use, perhaps slightly more advanced with their technology which made it look easier and quicker, and this is a must when dealing with time and tides.

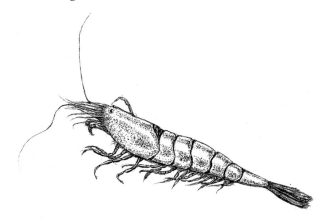

'THE BAY'

A hundred square miles of sea and sand,
The bay is quite unique.
It lies between the southern strand
Of the Lakes and our village creek.
A mercurial mix of water and land
In constantly changing state,
One moment it's there and the next it's gone
Like a flighty, tempestuous mate.

The bay has a dual persona,
One minute it's all sea and sky,
But next we know the sea's gone with the flow
And we're left with just sand in our eye.
Channels and quicksands come and go
In a wilderness unchanged by man.
In the past he has tried but the bay will decide
What future it holds, what it can.

Once in a lifetime the Kent will feel free
To change its direction and run,
Away from Grange and the northern range
Towards more Southerly fun.
It flows further south and into the mouth
Of the Lancaster channel in zest,
Past the shore and the Keer until it comes near
To Morecambe and Heysham for rest.

When I was a lad I saw postcards
Of steamers on Silverdale's shore,
Bringing trippers from Southport and Blackpool
To stay in our village and pore
Over natural beauty it offered,
Its woods and its marshes in spring,

And the birds and the squirrels and rabbits,
With the deer in Silverdale's ling.

In the days before railways were common,
The stagecoaches traversed the sands.
Morecambe to Ulverston was the route
For carriage and four-in-hands.
And cricketers playing in Barrow
Would race home ahead of the tide,
Across the broad bay at the end of the day,
Aglow with the win and their pride.

The shifting sands just come and go
As stealthy as owls in the night.
The fishermen know each ebb and flow
And times and tides that are right.
The whitebait nets in the bay are set,
Close to Silverdale's shore,
And tractors tow and fishermen blow
Till silvertails struggle no more.

From Flookburgh shrimpers set out for the bay
Early from village to shore,
The morning mist conceals their approach
As nets they unravel once more.
They trawl the bay's base at a slow walking pace,
Then empty their prize on dry sand.
And brown shrimps turn pink just as fast as you wink,
Far better than caviare grand.

And some days when watching the ebb of the bay,
A small army comes into view.
Mums and dads and girls and lads

In shorts and plimsolls new.
They're crossing the sands, their hearts in their hands,
A walk of four hours no less,
Across Keer and Kent until energy's spent
But warm with the glow of success.

Through stretches of water, some shallow, some deep,
They paddle and wade in turn,
Over ridges and bracks, through dykes with their packs,
Quicksand and jujubes they spurn.
Guided safely by Ced with his whistle and staff,
All dangers he seems to allay,
But the bay can deceive and he warns them at eve

To beware should they come back one day.
The sands never grieve and it's hard to believe
That the depths can be seventy feet.
And over the years there've been many tears
In homes where fishermen meet.
For dad's not come home and the roar of the foam
Can be heard at the heart of the bay.
And sorrow and strife was the catch for his wife
And his kids at the end of that day.

I hereby acknowledge and thank Mike Speak of Silverdale, LA5 0RZ for his permission to print this Poem.

POLLUTION PROBLEMS

We now have a totally different scene at this side of the bay, with high sandbanks being built up over the years and the river Kent so far away and so very little tidal movement. These combinations have been disastrous for the Grange side of the bay and added to that is the discharge from the sewerage works at Wyke Farm, Humphrey Head which provides a never-ending source of nutrients for the thriving Spartina which is spreading year by year.

I was not unduly worried in those very early days stages about 20 years ago, because I did not even know what Spartina was.

My access onto the sands, whether it was going fishing, taking a party of walkers, or groups of people on my 'sandpiper' rides was by crossing an area of very shallow water and this water seemed to be contaminated and some days it was every colour of the rainbow. At low tides sewage discharge was left stagnant for several days at a time and it really hummed in hot weather. There was just nowhere for it to go.

When the tide rose in height this sewerage was pushed back towards the shore and not taken out into the bay as one would think. The two farms nearest to the sands with low-lying land are Wyke and Wraysholme Tower. In long wet spells water drained away from these lands through a culvert under the railway line and out into the bay.

With the advent of this new sewage system now giving assistance to the build up of sand in this area meant that this waste was being prevented from running away into the bay and it started to build up on the land, making farming difficult if not impossible. These farmers rang me up one day to tell me of the situation and asked if anything could be done.

However the landowner came up with an idea, with which I did not agree and which proved to be very costly and was quite useless. It was thought that on very low tides man and machine could clear the culvert and dig a deep trench out into the bay. They did ask for advice from me but then ignored it and continued with the project. The shortest route was from the Wyke to the side of Humphrey Head, but there was quite a high area which was covered last by the high tides.

In a straight line from the Wyke to, say, Silverdale as the crow flies, the river must have been at least six to seven miles away, but the ebb and flow took that route. Every dyke and gulley ebbed back to the river which, as already mentioned, is the lowest part of the bay. The digger, man and machine worked hard and dug a long, quite deep trench over the shorter stretch towards Humphrey Head point

I had a good look at the trench after it was finished. It looked good, but as soon as the tides rose in height the trench was filled much more quickly than the time it took to dig it out It is very difficult to go against nature. There is now a permanent dyke which drains eastwards towards the river Kent.

At about that time I had a phone call from Group Captain Harry King, OBE who lived at Fleetwood asking if it would be alright if he came to see us at the farm. The subject was 'Pollution of the Bay'. He and many others were very worried when hearing the news that the N.W.W.A. had plans to bring Blackpool sewage north to Fleetwood, then taking it out to sea with the biggest pipe in Europe. This was putting it on someone else's doorstep, he said and was definitely going to do something about it. The average British outfall serves only 17,999 people. The Lune Deep outfall would be used on a daily basis by the hands, bottoms and other bits of 260,000 people plus Blackpool's million or more visitors during the summer. Nobody had ever pumped so much effluent into one place through one pipe before.

N.W.W.A. were conducting an experiment in OUR bay and they did not even know what was likely to happen in terms of sedimentation with an outfall on this scale..

This was the subject of our meeting with Harry King O.B.E. and it was suggested that a group be formed who were interested in doing something about this matter.

This was the start of our bid to save Morecambe bay and it was to be known as the 'Save our Bay Campaign (South Cumbria)'.

Our first public meeting was held in St Mary's Parish Hall, Church Walk, Ulverston on Monday, 6th February 1989. The panel was as follows:

Chairman:- Lieut.Commander J.M. Gale
Group Captain Harry King O.B.E.
Councillor Mrs W. Kalbe
Mr John Hutton
Mr Cedric Robinson
Councillor Richard Scott
Mr Norman Parker
Mr J.B. Holme

Agenda:-
1. Chairman's welcome and introduction. J.M.Gale
2. Background to Save our Bay Campaign and exposition on the Lune Deep Scheme. H.King
3. Exposition on the Ulverston scheme. W.Kalbe
4. Bathing standard and European Law. J.Hutton
5. Tides in the bay, flotsam, channel movements and effects on fishing. C. Robinson
6. Scientific Appraisal. C. R. Scott
7. Mechanics of the Campaign J.B. Holme
8. Questions – of which there were many - discussions and petition signing.
9. Chairman thanks Platform and Public.

At a later date a meeting was held at Holker Club, Cark-in-Cartmel and this was well-attended. After long studies by a team of experts a report was made and the committee came to the following conclusions as to the effect on the environment of Morecambe Bay by the proposed Fylde Coast long sea outfall:

1. The Bay is a shallow estuary which empties and fills with each tide and cannot be compared with the open sea.
2. The proposed discharge point for the outfall is located in the Lune Deep, which is the main channel feeding the bay on each side.
3. Morecambe Bay has recently seen a significant deterioration in its environmental quality and should be improved.
4. Studies by the Hydraulics Research Station have shown that water from the Lune Deep travels inland for considerable distances – i.e. as far as Lancaster on the Lune and Arnside on the Kent.
5. Non-tidal currents contribute to the movement of liquids and solids in the bay.
6. Sewage solids are highly mobile on the flood tide and are likely to accrete in the upper reaches of the bay.
7. There is an extremely worrying risk to public health from a build up of bacterial and viral levels in the bay.
8. The attempts by NWWA to model the effects of the outfall have been grossly inadequate in both method and scope.
9. The life of viruses in the turbid waters of the bay are far longer than has been assumed by NWWA.
10. There will be a major threat to the shellfish and tourists' industry in the area.
11. The proposals are in direct conflict to the forthcoming EEC legislation.
12. It is the opinion of this Society that the effects of the proposed long sea outfall in Lune Deep upon Morecambe Bay are potentially environmentally disastrous.

We were asked to keep on lobbying. Write to our local MPs, the Prime Minister, the European Parliament, the Duke of Edinburgh and Prince Charles and to the Secretary of State for the Environment - which we did.

I received a copy of the letter from Her Majesty's Inspectorate of Pollution the key paragraph of which stated:

On 5 March 1990, the Secretary of State announced that "...in future all significant discharges of sewage should be treated at a sewage treatment works before discharge to our estuarial or coastal waters." In view of this, the Secretary of State is unable to approve the applications before him based, as they are upon the discharge of untreated screened sewage. Furthermore, there is no existing treatment works that could be conveniently utilised to treat the sewage satisfactorily prior to discharge. The Secretary of State has therefore concluded that any further consideration of the applications and the representations, including the question of whether a local inquiry should be held, would not be appropriate. He accordingly directs the Authority to refuse it's consent to the proposed discharges.

GHOSTS AND LEGENDS

The Priory Dobbie deals with the ghost of a decapitated driver of one of the Mail Coaches which plied the Bay, the Priory woods and Sea Wood etc. was the home to a highwayman.

Sam Porter was a particularly nasty piece of work, who made a living holding up coaches and bsiness men crossing Morecambe bay.

A coach from Lancaster crossed from the Cartmel side to Conishead Bank adjacent to Conishead Priory. Sam Porter accosted the driver of the coach and demanded that the passengers, all well-to-do local people who were returning with their pockets full of cash after concluding various sales of goods to the warehouses of Lancaster. One of the passengers, a certain Mr White, pulled out his pistol and fired at Sam Porter, missing him. The irate Porter pulled the driver down from the coach and decapitated him in front of the scared passengers, at the same time demanding of them "Now you b...... empty your pockets into my hat or you will get the same".

Needless to say, they emptied their pockets and were allowed to go on their way. The dead driver was placed on the top of the coach and tied into the driver's seat. The horses were whipped into a gallop – went up the lane to the Priory and turned on to the the Bardsea – Ulverston Road at the western gates.

The ghost of the driver with his head in his hands is supposed to haunt the vicinity of Conishead Priory still.

The eerie wails of his voice and the sound of galloping horses hooves occur on moonlight nights during the summer.

PLUMPTON HALL LANTERN

At Plumpton Hall on the Ulverston side of the Leven sands there is a tale regarding a certain ancient lantern which hung in the Great Hall of Plumpton. Despite every effort to get rid of the lantern, it always returned to the same place in the house, despite having been thrown out onto the Ulverston sands. It seems that on the evening of the day that it was cast away ghostly footsteps, creaking of floorboards and rattling of doors occurred, together with a most sad voice of a woman wailing and crying as if her heart was fit to break was heard. The lantern always returned to where it hung from the ceiling. This phenonomen lasted for all the years the Proctor family lived at Plumpton.

Now the whole complex of the house and farm buildings has been built up with houses and flats and no-one knows what has happened to the 'Old Lantern'.

TRAGEDY OF THE 'ROSE QUEEN'

Further down the estuary where the bay widens out from Aldingham there is a true story of a dreadful fatality which took place out on the Ulverston sands in 1895.

A three-masted wooden schooner "The Rose Queen" was proceeding up the Leven channel to Ulverston, loaded with general cargo out of Whitehaven. The cargo consisted of a large number of barrels of tar. The ship caught fire and ran aground on the Moat Bank. Thomas Park Benson's father and his younger brothers ran up onto the Moat Hill gazing out to sea at a most horrific sight – the schooner was ablaze from stem to stern and all the crew of five were attempting to launch a row boat to escape from the inferno.

Sheer efforts were in vain and one by one the crew perished. Their screams of pain were heard over the water as the spectators on land watched helplessly at the terrible scene taking place before their eyes. Finally the last sailor perished and the ship with its cargo was burnt to the water line and sank.

Now it is said that on the anniversary of this calamity that the whole scene is recreated and the cries of agony from ghostly voices reach across the shimmering moonlit waters of the bay to those on land.

[Acknowledgement and appreciation of this story is extended to Mr Thomas Park Benson who lived in this area as a boy but now lives in Owen Sound, Ontario, Canada.]

FLOOKBURGH IN THE 20th CENTURY

Although Flookburgh is still only a village, development has gone on over the years, but at one time it was a Market Town and was given its first Charter by Edward I in 1278 under the Priory of Cartmel. Its second Charter was granted by Henry IV early in the fifteenth century, in 1412. This Document contained rights which were reaffirmed two and a half centuries later by Charles II on 8th December 1664, which gave grant to hold a weekly Market and a Fair at the same place every year, for three days duration on June 24th and on September 29th. Flookburgh at that time was probably the largest town in the district.

In its long history Flookburgh has seen tragic days. According to the Parish Registers of Lakeland the 'Black Plague' in 1598 and again in 1655 wiped out many families with great death toll. The survivors could not remove the dead to Cartmel but buried them in a mass grave in Eccleston Meadow. This particular meadow belonged in more recent years to Mr James Stockdale, and about the year 1887 he had the land drained and made level; he cut down two considerable mounds of gravel and clay which had been thrown up artificially, as if bodies had been buried there.

These disastrous plagues were followed by a further catastrophe in 1686 when a terrible fire demolished the greater part of the town. It occurred on the sixteenth of May that year, assisted by a mighty hot, dry wind, which reduced the town to the status of a village. The Villagers, as was the custom, applied to the Justice of the Peace to ask the King to grant a 'Brief' to be read in all the Churches and Chapels in the County, asking for collections to be taken to help the sufferers. After these catastrophes Flookburgh became merely a place of lodging for travellers crossing the sands, and later a fishing village, but still not without fear - about every twenty five years came monstrous high tides. These tides could rise, under certain peculiar circumstances far beyond all ordinary bounds, especially when the wind had been blowing furiously for days from the Southwest.

The highest tide was on the 27th December 1852, and though, by the tide-tables it was calculated as 16 feet six inches only, rose no less than three feet (perpendicularly) above any other tide ever before known, even by the oldest inhabitants of the village. Though the wind was a heavy gale on the 27th December that year, it did not begin to blow till about 7 am, on that day. Had there been a hurricane blowing for some days previously there would not have been the slightest doubt that the tide would have flowed up the old large drain into Eccleston Meadow and other low land below the Western part of Flookburgh, as it used to do in former days on some extraordinary occasions.

The sea at this time overlapped most of the sea embankments in the Parish of Cartmel. It covered all the low land in Holker Park, even within four or five hundred yards of Holker Hall, the lands at Bigland Scar, Old Park and Frith. Hay, and corn stacks at Old Park Farm stood in more than three feet of sea water. The road from Old Park Woods was covered by the sea, and small animals such as mice, rats and others had crept up into the trees and could be seen on both sides of the roadway. The tidal waters at Low Marsh House, Flookburgh, broke over the embankment, running up the ditches and actually entered into the cellar of the house at Myerside, where the drain already spoken of, leading from Eccleston Meadow and low land from Flookburgh, took the water towards Winder

Moor and back out to sea. It flowed thirteen yards up the road at Sandgate and overtopped all the shingle beaches, carrying many tons of gravel and even large stones into the fields. The action of the sea was so violent that it almost broke through the new embankment at East Plain Farm. At Foulshaw Mosses and other places, many sheep and cattle were drowned.

In the latter part of the eighteenth century when reclamation of marshy land was being planned by so many landowners, eyes were turned to the flat plains south of Flookburgh, between Humphrey Head and what was then called Cartmel Sands. Dykes had been built up in early times to protect the town from the sea, but when tides ran high, they came dangerously near to the edge, so that the householders heard the raging waters almost at their doors. Once a boat was brought with the tide and thrown by high waves into an orchard down the Croft. The name 'Croft' still stands in the village but the area has been developed recently into a housing estate, which is a short distance from the square, down past the village hall and Church Villas. The Square was the site of the old St John the Baptist Parish Church and, before land reclamation, was little more than a stone's throw from Flookburgh's old church. In 1776-77 the church had become so damp and ruinous that it was taken down and rebuilt, with a dedication to St John the Baptist. The new church of Flookburgh erected by the Duke of Devonshire in 1900, stands on the left hand side of the road between Flookburgh Square and the Railway Station.

In those early days Flookburgh was an independent, characteristic place, with most families following the sands for a living, men and women, with very few members of these families going in for trade. T'was only in latter years that fisherfolk started to leave the sands for a more stable situation with a reliable income. Although after 1849, educational opportunities for boys and girls did exist in the village of Flookburgh, schooling was still optional and many of the cocklers thought their children were better employed working on the sands than spending their time in school acquiring skills for which they saw no useful application.

From the thriving mill-towns of Lancashire and Yorkshire came continued demands for shellfish, giving the cockling families an opportunity to become a little better off, but sadly many were exploited. Although there were many fishing villages round the Bay, Flookburgh was the principal one, with at least 100 boys, girls and women going out onto the sands daily, sometimes twice a day. to collect cockles.

A Government enquiry into "The employment of Children, Young Persons and Women", looked at conditions locally in 1867 and much of the evidence recorded at that time was disturbing.

My father was born in Flookburgh in 1904 into a fishing family, as his father and grandfather before him bad been. Dad had two older sisters and a brother, and three younger brothers. He is now the only survivor of this family, but is very well himself and keeps remarkably fit for his age. He has lived in Flookburgh all his life, apart from a. short period when he was away fishing from Hambleton, near Poulton-le-Fylde, a small village alongside the River Wyre, and during the last war when he spent six years overseas in the Eighth Army. It was during his stay at Hambleton that he met my mother-to-be and they eventually married and moved back to father's native village and settled down, where his mother, brothers and sisters still lived.

Dad's sister Lucy, eldest of the family of seven, was able to recollect some of her very early memories in the village for me. At the age of three and a half years she started school, but her parents had to pay one old penny a week to the education authorities for her to attend. There were no school meals provided, so she and her pals would run home through the village for their dinners. No motor cars were ever seen, as everything was horse-drawn in those days. Holiday time from school was great fun, and amusement was taken by the girls with wooden hoops and for the boys, metal ones. These were called 'Booleys' and

Cedric's father, Bill Robinson, photographed when he was aged 96. (Nick Clark)

as you ran alongside you would strike the top of the booley with a wooden stick, or sometimes a metal one to keep it in motion.

As mentioned in the Arcadian Sketchbook, Flookburgh had a Church in the sixteenth century, which was rebuilt in the eighteenth century. This stood in the centre of the village, now the Square, and according to the inhabitants it was more like a barn than a Church. Bordering it was a stone wall with ornamental railings.

Lucy recalled that the older men of the village would always congregate at one end of the Church, outside the railings; this was called Chapel Corner, with all the men wearing similar dress, dark clothing, usually a suit, black shiny shoes, black gansey or a waistcoat. Most of them would be wearing a cap and smoking a clay pipe of 'bacca', . with some chewing it.

Fisherfolk, men and women, joined a club, whereby, if they ever became ill, they were able to draw half-a-crown a week from this (now 25 pence new decimal currency).

Whit Tuesday was always a great day for the village when a Club Walk was held with always a well-attended Procession through the village. One year a competition was held amongst all the fishermen to see who had the best groomed horse. Lucy's father entered their horse called "Polly", but it did not get a prize.

Flookburgh consisted of one long main street with the exception of Greenfield Terrace on Station Road. The top half of the village was Main Street, and the bottom half was Market Street. Village pubs were many and were open from six a.m. to ten p.m., with very little other activity in the village, although, before the first World War, women were never seen in a public house, and village life revolved around the Church. Girls were not allowed in Church without their head being covered, if only with their handkerchief, but most young girls wore bonnets - old fashioned bonnets which tied under their chins. They were not allowed to mix with the boys, so there would be a row of girls and a row of lads, with men at the back of the Church keeping an eye on them, to see that they behaved themselves. They were old enough to have done, but did not always do so; sometimes the lads would have a pea-shooter and every now and again a pea would fly past one's head or hit one's bonnet; then the lads would tease the girls and laugh and the fellows at the back of the Church, keeping an eye on the lads, would put all of them outside for misbehaving - all of them - including those who were innocent.

The young children would go to Sunday School in their best clothing, and nearly all the teenagers in the village went to evening service from six p.m. to seven thirty p.m. One of the pubs, the Crown now, in Market Street, operated the village's horse-drawn fire engine and the Landlord, also the owner and driver of the horses was Mr. John Mackereth, later the village coal merchant.

Parents were strict in those days and teenagers had to be home by eight p.m.. Women and young girls made their own clothes, and for working out on the sands, cockling in all weathers, they made their skirts out of unbleached calico and then treated them with several coats of linseed oil, which made them waterproof, and as these were the days before Wellington boots came into fashion, clogs were worn with their oiled skirts.

Before water was laid on in the village, people had to depend on pumps. There was one in the main street which went under the name of 'the town pump'. At night time all families would fill up their buckets with clear, fresh pump water. This would never run dry, but during the winter frosts it would freeze and someone would take a kettle full of hot water to thaw it out. Several houses in the village had their own pumps. Pump water was so very clear and cold and very good for washing the flukes, which would set, almost like being frozen and this would help to keep them, as there was no refrigeration in those days although, as they say, 'where there's a will, there a way'.

These fisherfolk smoked their own flukes from their cottage fireside. and also had a method of drying the fish by hanging them on clothes pegs above the fire, and when dry enough would store them in a cool place and make use of them for meals when no catches were available during winter months, and these were said to taste very good when cooked,

When all the fishermen, and these were many, arrived home from the sands, the village pump seemed to be in use all the day, washing their catches. Sunday mornings were also a busy time with all the fishermen taking their horses to the pump for a drink. Every household had a horse and cart, and some families had two. Fisherfolk knitted their own nets and made their own knitting needles from wood, but no-one went to the sands cockling or fluking on Saturdays or Sundays.

If a family were lucky enough to either rent or own a field, then their horse would be grazing out during the summer time, otherwise it was hard work for the many who did not have this opportunity. The grass verges had to be scythed between the tides, and the grass carted back to the stables to be fed to the sand horses. In wintertime they would be fed hay or 'chop', this being hay chopped very small by hand power. The hay would be fed along a shallow, open-topped wooden box and gathered through cogs which pressed the hay forward, and as it travelled along it was cut by two very sharp blades attached to the big circular wheel of cast iron which was turned by hand. This was good bulk feed for the hard-working horses, and with a little bran and a few oats added, there was never a poor hungry horse to be found in the village.

Within living memory the village was very much a self-contained community, relying on its own inhabitants to provide almost all the services required for the daily life of the people. It was a primitive way of life, with no running water supply and no electricity, and although the people of the village were poor at that time, no-one ever went hungry. There was one thing about the villagers, they were all in the same boat. Everyone was poor, but if one needed help it was always there, not for pay, but for a good turn done way back for some future date.

There were two blacksmith's shops in the village; one was Shuttleworths, up the main street with a good reputation as a farrier and he also took on all the shoeing of the horses at Holker Hall. The other, the Smithy down the village in Market Street was owned by two brothers, John and Peter Butler, and the same buildings today are used as a market garden and florists shop, but from these premises in those early days gone by, the two brothers were always kept busy with work from the fishermen, horse shoeing, and they specialised in making the crambs for cockling; a small metal, three-pronged fork; and not forgetting work from the farming community in the district.

Children would be fascinated watching the farrier lift the hot metal from the furnace and shape it on the anvil. Even in the village away from the smithy, one could hear the distinctive sound of the blacksmith's hammer tapping away on metal and anvil. This was a wonderful sight to see, and one particularly recalls the smell of the hot acrid smoke coming from the smithy when the farrier was seen shoeing a horse. The red-hot shoes, one at a time cut, shaped and then fitted when cooled, is an experience hard to find today. They had many other jobs to do besides shoeing horses. Often they would be asked to make some experimental piece of agricultural machinery, or design some special piece of wrought iron; and in the darker corners of the smithy you would find a strange assortment of implements long laid aside; old wheels, chains, hooks, all sorts of forgotten bygones – in fact a treasure trove of ironmongery.

Most of the carts used by the fishermen were made across the Bay at Silverdale. These were all of one type and easily recognised by the fishermen, being lighter than any other cart made in their own village of Flookburgh or the next village of Cark. Some carpenters were also wheelwrights, and always had plenty of work. Fixing the iron tyre or hoop on a cart wheel is an expert's job, but this could often be undertaken, not only by the wheelwright but also by the blacksmith.

A basket-maker in the village was always kept busy with regular orders from the fishermen for the cockle

Main Street, Flookburgh, in the days when it had still to receive a coat of tarmac. The old church with its railings is beyond the cart. At the bottom right is a jumbo at least 18 feet long. Used in cockling to bring the shellfish up to the surface, they cannot now by law exceed 4ft 6ins. (A.N. Wolstenholme collection)

baskets. These did not last for ever, as when cockle gathering, they get a certain amount of wear in the bottom with continuous movement along the sand, but to overcome this and give the cockle basket that little bit longer life, the fishermen would tack a narrow length of harness leather underneath to the 'bool' where the basket was forever in contact with the sand. The baskets were also soaked in tar and well dried before being put to use. This preserved them, adding quite considerably to their life-span.

These were the craftsmen of the past. The village tailor, carrying the materials and tools of his trade with him, would visit farms and cottages, to make suits and to repair work-worn clothes whilst sat at the kitchen-table. The village blacksmith, the tinker and the knife-grinder were regulars in those days. The saddler, though he still performed the primary task of his calling, would make leather braces, dog-collars and leashes and repair harness. In each of these trades is an accumulation of skills that have been handed down from one generation to the next.

In 1914 coal was a shilling per hundredweight., the equivalent of five pence in today's decimal currency. But an alternative was to use peat. My Father was only ten years of age at that time, but can vividly remember his family, along with other families from the village with horse transport, going along to Holker mosses and staking a claim, marking out an area with wooden stakes, cutting the peat and then leaving it to dry. No-one would ever steal from another person's claim. Money for this was paid to the Cavendish family at Holker Hall. The small outbuildings at the rear of a great number of village cottages, were called 'peat houses', and I suppose that name still sticks with many of them today.

When fishing was slack, the only way the menfolk could earn money was to go along to the 'Hiring Fairs', one of these being at Ulverston and taking place at Whitsun, for the six summer months and Martinmas , for the six winter winter months. Dad's first hiring was when his Mother took him at the age of twelve, together with his baggage, to Ulverston to get hired out onto a farm. As she left him she gave him a shilling (five pence in todays equivalent). He was hired to.a Mr Whalley Scott of Staveley, near Kendal, just outside that village. He stayed for about a week but could not settle, walking down into the village at night after work, but never meeting a soul. His boss could see that the lad was not settling but did not want him to leave. However, Dad had made up his mind and. although he considered both the farmer and his wife as being good sorts, at the first opportunity he would leave. As soon as the farmer yoked up his grey horse to take his butter and eggs to Ambleside, Dad left the farm for home. He walked all the way and got a good telling-off when he arrived. His father and his sister Mary left Flookburgh early next morning by horse and cart to Staveley to pick up Dad's box. Everyone in the village who got hired had these large boxes which they took with them. Dad said he didn't quite know why they were so big, because he only had a spare pair of trousers and two or three clean shirts with him.

One fisherman, whose wife was so houseproud that he was getting to the end of his tether, got himself hired out and never returned, as he had found a much better place!

Dad's second hiring was in his early teens when he was hired out in Giggleswick in Yorkshire. Other fishermen and their sons from the village were hired to the same area and in the evenings after work, or at weekends, they would arrange to meet in Settle and have a get-together. Lucy, Dad's sister, told me that Dad was always a good worker, and could work alongside any man, but he took it out of himself, and when he returned home, Lucy said he was as thin as a rake.

Still with little to be made on the sands, an opportunity came along which meant Dad would not have to leave the district. His Mother had heard that work was to start with the building of houses near to Flookburgh, now the village of Ravenstown. She told Dad to get himself down to Thompsons, the builders in Flookburgh, who at that time lived next door to the Co-operative Stores in Market street. The boss said to Dad, "what can you do", and Dad said "Oh, I can do owt", or something to that effect. They took him on and arrangements were made for him to be on the site first thing on Monday morning.

When Dad arrived for work there was Mr Thompson and his son, and the three of them started by building a toilet block before the building of the houses could go ahead. All the materials for the houses, wood, slates, bricks etc., came by train to Cark-in-Cartmel railway station from Barrow-in-Furness, then were carried from the railway station by horse and cart. In the stables down Moor Lane, now modernised and known as Stockdale Farm, there was stabling for fourteen fishermen's horses, and these fishermen helped by transporting the materials to the site. Later, as the building of the second half of the village progressed, a railway siding was built and a branch line was laid from the main line at Wrays Holme Crossing, near Humphrey Head. which came over the fields, across the bottom of Mireside Farm, over land which was formerly called 'The Goose Dubs', then alongside the cut to the lower or West side, of Ravenstown. "Oh aye" said Dad, "I remember when all that land was fields". Ravenstown, known at the time of its building during the first world war as Flookburgh West, was intended to house workers from an adjoining airship factory, but no sooner had the works been constructed than the scheme was cancelled. Messrs. Vickers of Barrow took over the houses which are now mainly owner-occupied.

I was also told by my father how men used to come round the villages with onions - roped onions. A railway wagon full of these would come to Cark railway station, and several men on bicycles had the task of peddling round villages for several days, with nearly every household buying these Spanish onions.

Another sight was when the Irish dealers came over by boat and brought with them at least one hundred` geese at a time.

These were small, dark-coloured geese and were flocked on foot from villages to farms, wherever a deal could be struck and a price bid for them.

Pianos were delivered into the village all the way from Ulverston by horse-drawn cart, and, as a lad coming home from school, Dad can vividly remember the Dancing Bears on chains performing in the village square. Quite a different village now, from what it was in those days, when people seemed to have had more time for each other.

Nowadays people seem to have more of everything except happiness. Almost everyone you meet in the village today is a newcomer. Gone are the days when women stood gossiping in doorways, children sat on doorsteps, and patient horses stood at stable doors.

When Flookburgh did come to life at varying hours of the day, according to the season and the tide-tables, long processions of horses and carts filed through the village to the cockle and fishing grounds, some down Moor Lane, others to Sandgate and out onto the sands.

To assist the livelihood of these fishing families who depended so much on the sands of Morecambe Bay, they would set nets to catch sea-birds, these being mainly Oystercatchers and the 'dowker' - a small duck. The shore at Sandgate used to be black with these birds, and the fishermen caught them in large quantities. Dowker nets were set on the sands near Chapel Island, at that time called Chapel Bed. This was a large area with good feeding grounds, with young shellfish and tiny whea'at, (young cockles), which encouraged the birds to feed. Wooden stakes about four feet in height were worked down into the sand. The nets were attached to these stakes to lie horizontally about two feet above the surface of the sand. When the tide covered the sands, the ducks would dive down and feed, and when they surfaced they would become entangled in the meshes of the nets.

Setting nets to catch sea-birds is no longer allowed as they are now protected by law.

Samphire picking was also carried out by the fishing-folk and Dad told me that, out from Sandgate to the West

(Above) Flookburgh men and women in leggings and clogs, photographed on the Silverdale foreshore in the early 1900s.
(Lower) The oldest house in Flookburgh – with a 1665 datestone above the doorway. It has just been renovated.
(A. N. Wolstenholme collection)

side of Flookburgh, near to Cowpren Point, was an area of at least five acres of lush green Samphire as long as your hand. Samphire is a marsh plant, a coloniser on mud flats, estuaries and shallow coasts. Drowned by high tides twice a day, scorched by the sun, it grows bright green in the Summer and wine red in the Autumn.

The larger specimens grow woody stems, so the more tender, succulent plants are the younger, small ones. It is delicious to eat and people often compare it to asparagus. In fact the villagers called it 'Poor man's Asparagus'.

The Botanical name for Marsh Samphire is Salicornia stricta. Delicious as a vegetable, most people simply boil it after washing it well in fresh water to remove the excess salt. Boiled for about three minutes, this would then be served with lots of butter as a starter or as a main vegetable. It could also be pickled in vinegar.

Samphire bruises easily, so care was taken by the fisherfolk as they washed their harvest, which was then bagged in hessian sacks, sewing the tops of the bags with needle and string. This was then generally sent by rail to the wholesale fish merchants on commission, but the returns were very poor indeed, as these people took advantage of and exploited the fishermen, but at least it did help augment their income, which was very low, with cockles at that time selling for only three or four 'Bob', (15pence or 20 pence), per hundredweight.

The Samphire still grows around our shores in Morecambe Bay, but no longer is it gathered and sent off to the market and mill towns of Lancashire and Yorkshire, where the people had a great liking for this succulent vegetable.

Perhaps the greatest tribute to any districts past is the interest shown by later generations. Modern progress and development has now reached out from the towns and cities to the many villages in this area, but if it cares to look around they may well find many things of interest from those by-gone days.

The name of a village may convey some idea of its origin. Flookburgh, possibly named from the much sought-after Fluke or Flatfish caught in Morecambe Bay, is an example.

Fluke or Flook may be from the Norse name 'f loki', which also means flatfish. Most Flookburgh folk would like this to be true, as they believe that the weather-vane on their Church is a representation of a flatfish, but most of the fishermen, including myself, think this to be an Angler fish, (Lophius piscatorius).

Flukes are still caught in the Bay in much the same way as they were centuries ago but, sadly, demand for these tasty flatfish is very poor in recent times.

Modern housewives prefer their fish ready prepared, either fresh or packed for the modern freezer. It is only the fishermen and their families, and perhaps a number of the villagers, who still buy the flukes fresh to be either dipped in flour, fried, then eaten on the bone, which is much the tastier way, or to buy them ready filleted, pan-fry them in a little oil, microwave them in milk or butter for two to three minutes, or to deep-fry them in batter. The fish are really delicious whichever way they are cooked. These filleted flukes are only available, as a general rule, from the fishermens premises when a prominent sign is usually displayed, at an unbelievable price range for these days, of between £1 .00 to £1.20 per pound ! Hard to understand but perfectly true.

No more will the men of Flookburgh bring home three thousand tons of cockles per year, selling at about forty eight shillings per ton, (£2.40 now). These were regular figures in the latter years of the nineteenth century.

Although Morecambe Bay is so vast and cockle beds can spread over such huge areas, there is a skill in finding the best beds and fishermen out in the Bay were always trying to get the better of one another. None were really pals when they were out there working, and if a good patch of cockles was found it was kept secret from the others. The area would only be visited in the dark, tide permitting, and they would work hard on it before the rest of the fishermen realised what was happening.

As soon as the tide ebbed and the higher sandbanks

showed, the oystercatchers and the gulls made their way down to the cockle beds in large numbers - then the fishermen also had to be on the move.

The fisherfolk were not totally immune to the dangers of the sands and sadly, over the years, many deaths have been recorded. Amongst them are the following:

In 1829, on November 19th, a woman named Ellen Speight was gathering mussels on Heysham sands when she was surrounded by the tide and drowned. In 1843, on March 16th, three fishermen from Bolton-le-Sands, William Woods , James Dickinson and John Woof were all drowned by the tide whilst out fishing. They were all married men, and a subscription was arranged for their widows and seven children.

Two of the worst disasters in crossing the sands are reported in the "Lancaster Records", with a total loss of twenty-two lives. The first, which occurred on 4th June 1846 was the loss of nine persons drowned while crossing Ulverston Sands, and in 1857 some young men, thirteen in number, were crossing the Kent sands on their journey from Flookburgh to Lancaster Fair. Their horse and cart plunged into a deep hole near to Priest Skier and the River Keer, and all thirteen were drowned.

An old Morecambe fisherman told me the story of a disaster which happened on the sands. A cockler, his wife and their two grown-up daughters were out on the sands when a thick fog came down. The cockler left the cart to see if he could recognise anything which would help him find the way home but he never returned to them. After waiting for some time the women were overtaken by the tide, so they let the horse have its head to go wherever it wished. The mother was washed off the cart and drowned, but the horse, sometimes wading and sometimes swimming, eventually brought the two daughters safely back to the shore.

Jimmy Stephenson from Flookburgh was drowned on the sands not far out from Humphrey Head. He used to walk out with a cockle basket over his shoulder and gather a few cockles, then on his return, he would hawk them around the villages of Allithwaite and Cartmel to make a bob or two. Septimus Benson and his father from Flookburgh had been out on the sands with their horse and cart to fish a 'bawk' net for flukes. On their way home they remembered seeing Jimmy walking out, but never thought anything about it, as he was often seen out there. On this occasion he had stayed out on the sands too long and was cut off by the tide and drowned. His brother Kit was at that time working with other fishermen on the Kent railway viaduct which was being repaired. As the tide ran through the viaduct, Kit noticed a cockle basket floating along on the fast-running tide, and guessed that it was his brother's. Sadly it was, and Jim was drowned on that tide. He was the younger brother of Tommy and Kit Stephenson of Flookburgh. Tommy and his wife Maggie lived in one of the cottages behind the Market Cross, and Kit and his family lived in Market Street. I believe Tommy and Maggie were the first couple to be married in the new St. John the Baptist Church at Flookburgh.

WARTIME IN FLOOKBURGH

It was wartime, dad was away in the army and although I was very young, I was the man of the house and very close to my two sisters Peggy and Jean. I always looked after Jean as she was the youngest and mam had to go out to work to make ends meet.

Part of the time mam went cleaning for a lady called Mrs Smith who lived over the railway bridge at Piggy Town, a small community where there was a Church and a bakery owned by Mr Hughes. This lady used to go away at weekends on the train and I had to carry her suitcases to and from the station.

My sister Jean would watch me with these two big heavy suitcases and my reward for this work was a penny. As it was coming up to Christmas time I was expecting a treat but was so disappointed; she gave me a little calendar which I gave to Jean. She loved it - it was very tiny with blue violets on the front and she treasured it for years.

I did not like going to school although my sisters seemed to enjoy it. We would come home from school to a warm fire in a black iron grate and make toast on big long toasting forks, then we would play draughts and dominoes and snakes and ladders. I always used to let my sisters win. This was usually during the winter months when we had the really, really dark evenings. There was no street lighting as there is today.

On wet days mam would give us a penny to go on the bus to Cark. We put on our 'macs and wellies', then we walked back home to Flookburgh, jumping and splashing in as many puddles as we could find.

When it was fine in the summertime we wandered for miles through the fields with our little terrier dog called 'Crackers', picking bunches of wild flowers and, when they were in season, blackberries and elderberries for jam-making. Most of the fields round Flookburgh have dykes (ditches) around them and my sister Jean could not always jump them so I would cut big branches out of the hedge for her to scramble across. Sometimes we found 'watergollens' (marsh marigolds) - lovely yellow flowers and also watercress in these dykes.

Once, we were picking these watergollens under "t' willie-brig" (Willow Bridge) down Moor Lane from the village along mile road as locals call it, when we saw this huge water rat. I don't know who was most frightened, it or us.

When the farmers were laying their hedges (dyking) we used to take a sack and collect all the little bits of wood. I think we must have taken some out of the hedges because I remember one farmer chasing and shouting at us. I think it was a Mr Satterthwaite from Applebury Hill Farm as we were up this lane round the Green Lane.

Once we were in Harold Edgar's field when the sirens went off very loudly and German aeroplanes came over so we hid in the hedgerow thinking we would be safe but our little dog Crackers kept running into the middle of the field barking. We were terrified it was going to get bombed. I think we were out mushrooming that day but Harold Edgar used to chase us for climbing on his wall trying to reach walnuts from his tree near the farm. Jean used to sit on the wall, whilst I jumped into the field to pick up the nuts off the ground and Jean looked out for the bull which the farmer kept in the field. I wonder if that tree is still there?

We also got chased by Lord Richard Cavendish once when we were collecting nuts in the grounds of Holker Hall estate - right in front of the Hall - when we heard someone coming on horseback. So we jumped on our bike (two on a bike) and pedalled like mad but he came galloping after us. He stopped us and told us to walk as cycling was not allowed in the park. He never mentioned the nuts we had down our jumpers which were bulging and all our pockets were full too.

We also used to cycle down to Humphrey Head to the bluebell wood and pick the bluebells and primroses. We would go and cup our hands and have a drink at the Holywell and then climb up to the cave where the 'last wolf' was supposed to have been killed.

My sister Jean always wanted to take some pebbles home from the beach, but I would never let her do that as I said that was stealing. The beach belonged to the Royal Family.

However, there was a time when we were blackberrying in Whiteman's field, Mireside, when we found a nest of hen eggs in a haystack away from the farm, next to a pond, so we filled our cans with eggs, then covered them over with blackberries. We did this about once a week for quite a long time and this was not easy because we had to pass the "haunted house" to get there. I can just remember the person who lived there on his own - his name was "Jobe Johnston". Because it was wartime and food was rationed we thought it was worth taking the risk and the eggs were a real treat.

Mother once bought a flitch of bacon on the 'black market' from a woman who kept pigs in her backyard. We put it in Jean's doll's pram and put dolls on top of it and wheeled it home. Jean had lots of rag dolls because mam made them and sold them all round the village at Christmas time. She bought the 'faces' from the Post Office and we all sat round the fire cutting up rags all night to stuff the dolls with. Mother also made lovely velvet elephants and these were my favourites. Our fingers became sore and often the skin would blister because we used the scissors for such a long spell. I wonder if anyone in the village still has any of these lovely elephants. Mrs Burrow, who lived next to the butcher's shop, had two daughters, Mina and Joan, and she always bought these elephants for the two girls.

Once a day I had to take our horse out of the stable to the watering place (town dyke) so I would put a folded sack on its back and sit Jean on it, tie her feet together under its belly and she would slide round underneath it. Then I would laugh saying she could not fall off! We used to play for hours down there building dams.

During the war years the siren was a most frightening sound. The home guard were on duty in the village and with dad being away they used to come and take mam and us children to the air raid shelter. Our next door neighbour was Johnny Wright and he always went down the road with us to the shelter as this was very frightening. You could hear the bombers overhead and you could see the searchlights trying to pick them out and once, between our house and the shelter a bomb had dropped. It was pear-shaped, about the size of an oil-drum but it had not gone off so the home guard were defusing it and the impact of the bomb had made a huge crater. The air raid shelter was a large concrete building underneath the Electricity Board's yard with concrete seats built all the way round. Whilst in the shelter we used to sing all the old songs until the home guard came along and gave us the all-clear and took us home. After the war the yard and premises were bought by a local chap named "Pop (Robert) Benson" and this was called 'Stockdale' farm.

I rememberr going along to see a huge crater in a field near Humphrey Head and that particular bomb must have exploded because this huge hole spread over two fields.

Another time we all, that is almost everyone from the village trooped round Green Lane to see a German aeroplane that had come down in a field just above the Green on Applebury Hill, but it was cordoned off and we were not allowed to touch it – it had nosedived into the side of the hill.

Judge Alsebrook lived in a large house at the Green and I think he was the only person in the village with a car. It was open-topped and on a Sunday after Church he

Flookburgh fishermen trawling for shrimps in the early 1950s. (A.N. Wolstenholme)

would load us kids into it and take us all to his home and give us all a glass of fresh warm milk from his Jersey cow.

I remember going to Allithwaite the day after it had been bombed. A bomb had been dropped in front of a row of houses in Holme Lane going up the hill out of Allithwaite towards Grange-over-Sands. It had taken away the front of every house in the row. All the beds and furniture were hanging as if just balancing from the bedroom floors. It was thought to have been a stray bomb dropped as the Germans were trying to hit the shipyard at Barrow-in-Furness. Barrow was bombed very heavily that night. Older people in Allithwaite still remember. Mrs Brockbank, who used to entertain audiences with her poetry in local dialect, wrote an account of it.

We all had our own gas masks to take to school with us and my sister Jean had a Mickey Mouse one, but although we rehearsed wearing them at school we never had to use them in an emergency.

One particular time I remember setting out, this time with my elder sister Peggy on dad's big bike, two on a bike to Humphrey Head. My sister wanted to pick flowers and I would go along for company. I really cannot recall now whether I rode on the crossbar or sat on the handlebars, but off we set. By this time we had got more accustomed to the sound of the aeroplanes as we had the aerodrome down the Mile Road and target practice took place from the Army camp (which is now the Lakeland Leisure Centre). We cycled off, singing and giggling but we did not dare tell mam as she would have worried herself to death about us and it was strictly out of bounds to be there if the red flag was flying from Humphrey Head. This fine summer evening we were lucky - or so we thought.

We scrambled up the sheer face of the Head, over the top and then over the high wall into the woods. It was lovely. Peggy said it was like another world. We thought we were the only ones in that wood, except for the birds and the flowers. There were bluebells, primroses, dogramps everywhere, and we seemed to pick so many, I wondered however we would get them home on dad's big

bike. Then suddenly we saw it, this big shiny thing and as Peggy pulled the flowers back it was there - a large silvery shining bomb, shaped like a torpedo!.

Peggy grabbed hold of me and we both ran as fast as we could, scrambling over the wall as we were so frightened that this bomb would explode. Peggy knew what it was as only the week before, our local policeman 'Blackout Joe' had been at the school and given a lecture on the subject of bombs, so this made us even more frightened. This bomb was found to be live and very dangerous, but was eventually dealt with and made safe by the Army.

My younger sister Jean was very young when dad was called up into the Army and he was away from home for almost six years. She did not recognise dad when she was walking to school with her friends. I was coming down the road with my dad in uniform. Jean's friends pushed her towards us saying "Go on, Jean, it's your dad coming home from the war - then she rushed towards us. He picked her up and carried her home and I proudly carried his kitbag.

We were allowed that week to be away from school and dad had brought bars of dark chocolate with a layer of milk chocolate through the centre which he gave to us, our friends and all the kids in the row. Jean thinks that was the first chocolate we ever had.

When I was about eight years old my two cousins from Glasson Dock, Gladys and Renee came to visit us and wanted to take me back for a holiday with them. They bought me a little toy pipe, it was yellow and brown – I shall never forget it. They were teaching me how to smoke by putting their fag ends into it and getting me to puff it. I was very sick and poorly and had to be brought home. I have never ever smoked since.

When I was a bit older I was supposed to go to the school clinic at Ulverston on the train with a school friend, Bobby Jarvis. His parents were the licencees of the Hope and Anchor Hotel at Flookburgh. Instead of going to the clinic we went down to the Ulverston Cattle auction and

Then and now.
(Top) Market Cross, Flookburgh. (A..N.
Wolstenholme collection)
(Lower) The village's Main Street in February
1996 after a heavy snowfall.

spent the time looking round at all the animals which were being offered for sale. When the time came for catching the train and going home we threw our clinic cards out of the train window as the train rattled over the river Leven railway viaduct. The next day I was not looking forward to going to school but I had to and face the consequences which were dire. My pal and I were both given the cane and it didn't half hurt but it probably taught us a lesson. That was the first time I had done wrong and believe me, it was the last!

My pal Bobby had a nanny goat, which was black and white with horns. Most people thought it was a billy goat and we used to have hour upon hour of fun with this animal. We used to yoke it up into the cart which was a homemade bogie, a box type affair with shafts and mangle wheels and we used rope to make the harness. When it was wet and water stood in the hollows of the local fields, we would set off as happy as sandboys, then take the goat through the water and pretend we were fishermen catching shrimps. The goat was not too pleased at times when we took her up to her belly in the water.

We had a great idea – we had heard that someone in the village of Cartmel had a billy goat and we thought that we would like some baby goats (kids). We set off one day, the two of us, with the goat on a halter. By gum! It did seem a long way. We took it to be served by this lady's billy goat. She wanted us to leave the nanny goat with her and asked us to come back the following week.

When we went back to Cartmel for the goat she said that it had not come into season, but she wanted to charge us for its keep. I do not think we ever paid that lady but I know that we never went near to her place again.

Animals were always on my mind so I started to go regularly before and after school to George Dickinson's racing and livery stables at Cark-in-Cartmel. I remember feeling so proud of myself in a new suit with long trousers. Mother told me not to go near the horses on this day as I was dressed up. Amongst other lads I was offered a ride from the stables out to the fields, an offer no-one could

refuse. Riding full gallop up this lane, higgledy piggledy when the horse stopped suddenly at the gateway to the field. Well, I went straight over the horse's head and landed in a dub of dirty water. I got leathered when I got home but this did not deter me from going again to the stables.

Our house which was number four was in the middle of a row behind the ancient Market Cross opposite the Hope and Anchor Hotel with a backyard opening onto the village square. Two small rooms upstairs, two down with no electricity upstairs so we used candles. All the houses shared a tap in the backyard; we did not have a bath and shared an outside toilet with the old couple next door, Nanny and Faddy-Tom Stephenson and their son, Clem.

There were three outside toilets between the six houses. We used to cut up squares of newspaper and thread them onto string and hang them up in the toilet. There were no toilet rolls then! There was a little square hole in the wall in which we put the candle when it was dark. It was all so very scary in the dark.

Opposite each back door of the cottages was a wash-house where we kept the coal and a washing boiler where mother did the washing and boiled the water to put in a tin bath in front of the fire for us all to have a bath. Outside each wash-house was a mangle and a dolly-tub. On wet days, in the doorway of the wash-house we put up a swing made out of rope and a short piece of wood for the seat and had many hours of fun from this. The yard was cobbled and mam used to pour boiling water between the cobbles to kill the weeds. The washing was hung across the yard to dry.

I remember getting a lovely big white furry rabbit after spending weeks making a hutch for it. The hutch was set up from the ground on stone blocks and this seemed ideal. The very next day I was up very early and went outside to feed this lovely rabbit and there was white fur everywhere. My cat had got to it and killed it. Never again did I keep a pet rabbit but I still thought a lot of 'mi' cat.

When dad started fishing again just after the war

with horse and cart, he knew I was a good help to him and quite capable of looking after his horse – that is, grooming, feeding and taking it to water at the town dyke, as we called it.

As time went on I reached the age of 14 years and left school with only one thing on my mind and that was to follow the sands of Morecambe bay for my livelihood as my Father, Grandfather and Grandmother had done before me.

I was working with horse and cart gathering the cockles, mussels, shrimps and flukes – the tasty flat fish similar to plaice but superior. Cockling to me seemed the hardest job as this was done mainly in the winter months and the weather at times was bitterly cold as the harsh winds penetrated the warm clothing which we were always told to wear – wrap up well as we would be out on the sands for several hours at a time. Fishing was a hard life, even for the older fishermen – but hard work never killed anyone as my dad would say. However, the wind out there could be really cruel at times.

Most of my school pals left school to go into a trade such as a joiner, builder, plumber etc. but fishing was never classed as trade. All the same, I knew what I wanted to do and was keen to follow the sands as that was what really interested me.

Dad would explain to me how to read the tides and about the movement of dykes and gullies etc.on the sands and how to set nets to catch the flukes and other fish.

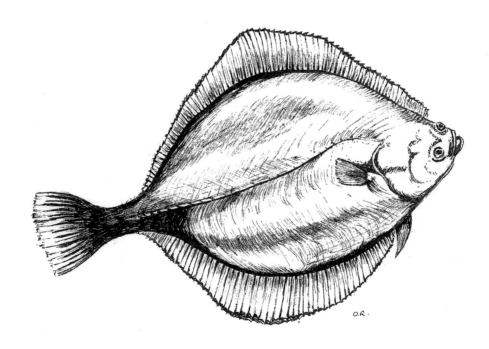

THE ROYAL CARRIAGE CROSSING
30th May, 1985

I had guided thousands of people across the treacherous sands of Morecambe Bay, but I would be tackling something new on Thursday, 30th May by guiding horse-drawn carriages across the bay in the first attempt for possibly over a hundred years AND more likely than not, H. M. the Duke of Edinburgh would be sitting besides me in the leading carriage on this epic journey.

This crossing was the idea of the Estate Manager of Holker Hall, Mr David Lee, and the journey would be made between Silverdale on the Morecambe side of the bay to Kents Bank on the Grange-over-Sands peninsula.

The four-mile trip is particularly hazardous because of a very fast tidal flow into the bay. I was there to make sure it was not going to be dangerous, as it was a matter of knowing what we were doing and which way to go on the day.

This event would need some special thought and preparation. It was being sponsored by Tetley Walker.

Time was moving very quickly towards this great event. It was only a matter of three weeks to the day of the Carriage Crossing, and conditions were very uncertain. All the weeks of planning; studying of tides and tide-tables, of weather forecasts and watching the movements of the river and gullies, to say nothing of the headaches as the river altered course yet again, and the added worry of the continual rain.

Would it clear in time to leave the sands hard enough for these narrow wheeled vehicles? It had a lot to do in a very short time, but I could only wait and hope that things would improve. In the meantime, enquiries were being made around the picturesque village of Silverdale for a suitable meeting place for the drivers and the vehicles carrying their horses and carriages.

This meant somewhere with a good access for large vehicles and preferably as near to the shore as possible.

After several visits to the area by myself and later by Mr Hugh Cavendish and Mr Lee from Holker Hall, the ideal place was found on the outskirts of the village. Stone Bower Fellowship Home for the Elderly Disabled, in Cove Road. This was a quiet, secluded place with a small meadow at the rear, but large enough for the needs of this occasion. Mr Bernard Wood, Manager of the Home was only too pleased to be involved, and willingly gave permission. From here there was good access to the shore only a short distance down Cove Lane. Straight ahead was a good firm route which years earlier had been laid with hardcore for the benefit of local men working tractors and trailers loaded with sea-washed turf.

At first sight this was thought to be ideal by the organisers, but they had not ventured out onto the sands and just thought it looked alright. At the time, the tides were low and had been for the last few days. Also, the weather was fine and the sand near the marshland had dried out, giving the impression that they were safe. This was not so, as discovered several days later, when I travelled round to Silverdale to re-check this route. The weather had changed. The tides had risen in height and I found the whole area unsuitable when I walked over it...I was not too disappointed at this, as I had an alternative route in mind, and also had prior knowledge of the whole area, from the walks I had done from Silverdale to Kents Bank near Grange-over-Sands.

This route was a rather uneven way out across the marsh with deep holes and nasty gullies. Where the marsh met up with the sands there was also a pretty steep drop. Although the depth of this varied within a foot or so in places, the sand level must have been at least four feet lower than the grassy marsh. Now, although I was able to negotiate these areas with the walkers on the sands, I had to think about some improvements and work out how to go about this before the carriage drive on the thirtieth of May. I was in constant touch with the organisers and we decided that to make a good job of it we needed someone out there with a J.C.B. mechanical digger to fill in the holes and do patching up work here and there. Finally, we would need to make a wide ramp with sand. Now of course before setting out to find someone willing to do the work we first had to get permission from the owners of the marshland i.e. the R.S.P.B. at Leighton Moss Nature Reserve at Silverdale, and this was readily given. I was soon to find Mr David Singleton from Tewitfield, Carnforth and his son Peter who came later to carry out the work, which was done to our entire satisfaction.

Before the work was started we arranged to meet and walk out on to the sand and look over the area. Mr Singleton could not foresee any problems, but he pointed out to me the weight of his machine.

When we came to the later and most important piece of work - the making of the ramp down onto the sands - I assured him that it would be quite safe. However he insisted that I came along and supervised. I agreed to this but I also knew that it would be a complete waste of his time and mine if this work was carried out too soon. The tides would just have washed all the sand away. I decided that the work must be carried out on the day before the Carriage Crossing, when the tides were at their lowest. We had to gamble on the weather and just hope that it would stay fine. The problem of the ramp now solved, we made our way back to where we had left our cars and arranged to meet again on May 29th to carry out the work.

Things were progressing slowly and the only worry at the moment was the weather.

Tetley Walker, the North-west Brewery Company was sponsoring both the Kent River Crossing on May 30th 1985 and also the Holker Driving Trials and County Show following the Crossing of the sands. There had been press meetings held at Holker Hall, but as yet nothing had been released to the public. There had been no official announcement up to date that the Duke of Edinburgh would take part in the drive over the sands.

The Police, the local Chief Coastguards, John Duerdon from Arnside, Don Shearer from Walney and myself were informed of any progress at these meetings. A News Information sheet had been compiled for the press by Brian Johnson the Tetley Walker Public Relations Officer in Manchester. Everything was in hand, waiting for confirmation from Buckingham Palace, and until this was forthcoming everything had to be kept under wraps.

It was Tetley Walker's fourth year of sponsorship of the events at Holker Hall, and coincided with the tenth anniverary of the three-day event staged at Holker Hall, the Stately Home of the Cavendish family. This event is held yearly at the first weekend after the Bank Holiday.

When it was officially announced that the Duke of Edinburgh was to take part in the drive over the sands I was informed by Mrs Johnson of Holker Hall and the following day by the B.B.C. Television from Manchester. A brief interview was needed for a news item. Following this, the press, the T.V. companies and the local radio stations were very, very interested. From then on, our telephone was ringing incessantly, right up to the day of the drive.

Lots of people were concerned about the horses, thinking it was too dangerous and what would happen if some of them were to go down in quicksands! When I was available to answer the telephone I assured them that the horses would come to no harm and would be all the better for the drive over the sands. The number of carriages had been limited to twenty and in the event there were some drivers who had second thoughts.

I also told these people that when horses were used regularly out there in the bay by the Flookburgh fishermen, including myself, although it was hard work for them at times, they were always fed well and the salt water did them good, improved their joints and there was never a poor horse to be seen out on the sands. This seemed to put their fears at rest. Others were worried on my behalf. Many calls were from people inquiring where the drive was to start out and how long the drive would take. Others wanted to know where I would be bringing them ashore.

I had been warned by the Police to contact them immediately if I had any suspect calls, but all the calls were genuine.

Before long, I was to meet up with the organisers from Holker and representatives of Tetley Walker including the driver of the two Shire horses at the Kents Bank Hotel. This meeting was to put them in the picture a little bit more about the sands, the river Kent and the route I had in mind.

After a drink and a bite to eat it was decided we should make our way down to Kents Bank Railway Station and take a look at the railway crossing and walk down the ramp onto the sands. The day was fine, the tides low and the sands could not have looked better. Proposals were put forward and decisions taken and we all came away feeling that we had achieved something out of this meeting.

Tetley Walker, the sponsors, arranged to put their banners on the beach and posts were put in which served the dual purpose with the thirty foot banners, of keeping the crowd under control.

I was asked if I would draw up a map of the route and have it at the Kents Bank Hotel on the morning of May 30th for the briefing of the press. This I did for them with the help of my wife Olive.

It was now Wednesday, May 15th, and I had previously arranged to take Melvin Bragg, (now Lord Bragg) of T.V. fame, across the sands on Saturday, May 18th, from Hest Bank to Kents Bank, Grange-over-Sands. It was to be an afternoon walk. He wanted to pick up a few facts about the bay and its history for a new book he had in mind, "The Maid of Buttermere". I also thought that this would give me the opportunity as there were only the

two of us, for me to relax but also at the same time to take note of the sands and especially of the river Kent crossing.

As arranged I met up with him on the foreshore at Morecambe Lodge Farm, Bolton-le-Sands and the day could not have been a better one. We set out in brilliant sunshine and this made the walk most enjoyable. Melvin Bragg was a very interesting person and we got on well together. One thing that surprised him out there was the vastness of the bay. The flow of the river Kent was swift and he remarked here of the danger. He found it difficult to keep his balance and seemed so glad when we reached the other side. It took us four and a half hours to cross the bay and when I asked him how he felt after the long walk he admitted to being tired. Although he was used to walking long distances on the hills in the Lake District he agreed that this walk over the sands was entirely different, but very enjoyable. He wrote a full account of it in The Punch Magazine of which I was sent a copy along with a letter of thanks.

My wife Olive always takes a keen interest in the bay walks and the conditions out there so with the carriage crossing only twelve days ahead, we were both keeping our fingers crossed for good weather and firm sands, to help make this a safe crossing for everyone.

This historic drive over the sands did pose security, crowd control and traffic problems for the two police forces, Lancashire on the Silverdale side and Cumbria at Kents Bank and Grange-over-Sands. I myself had spent long, anxious hours on the sands plotting a safe route, only to find the sands shifted by every tide.

The police were obviously interested in what was going on out there in the bay and I had frequent telephone calls asking me whether the drive was still on. The weather was now bad with heavy rainfall and high tides. This combination contributed to the changes in the river Kent and at this stage looked like putting the crossing in jeopardy.

Another telephone call from the police in Kendal. I was out on the sands at the time so Olive took their number and asked if I would ring them back when I reached home. This I did and they wanted to know whether this whole event could be a last minute decision. "Yes" was my reply and from that he said "You'll understand Mr Robinson, that you have only to look after the Duke of Edinburgh while he is on the sands. We have the job of looking after him for the whole of the time he is up here in the area". Well, I really did not know what to say to that: It was certainly a busy time for all of us and we were all so looking forward to this event. We were hoping and praying for some kind of miracle to happen out there to improve the conditions and make the drive across the sands possible.

Time seems to go by much quicker when you are kept busy, but I was now feeling a little despondent after long hours out on the sands with very little to show for it. It was of no use marking out a route as the place chosen to cross the river one day was quite impossible the next day. I estimated that the river Kent moved between four and five hundred yards each day. What I decided on was to organise the cutting of the brobs (laurel branches) for marking out the route as we should need quite a number of these. I was lucky to have some good friends on both sides of the bay, who were only too keen to give me a hand. George Riley from Bolton-le-Sands, Mr John Duerdon, Chief Coastguard from Arnside and several of his auxiliaries came out as far as the river Kent with me on the final day of marking out the route. Dick Proctor and Kath from Silverdale gave me their help and from this side John Barber and my son-in-law Chris worked with me.

It is said that when you are in need of something desperately, you can never lay your hands on it right away This apparently was the case because here at Guides Farm until recently we had a good length of hedge which was all laurel bushes slightly overgrown with age. These I cut to mark out the river crossings during the summer walks and as markers to the cockle grounds in the murky and foggy winter months as they had been used by my predecessors over many years. Unfortunately, some enthusiastic road

workers laying large pipes for the new sewage system from Grange-over-Sands to Humphrey Head decided that it would be to their advantage if they lopped the laurels down almost to ground level. This now posed a problem for me which I had never faced before. I had decided that when the time was right we would start the marking out from the Silverdale side, this being the lower part of the bay and the most dangerous on the route. This would allow us less working time than on the Grange side where the sands rose up much higher to form firmer and safer sands. All was dependent on the weather to make this big occasion a success. After listening to the daily weather forecasts, many of which were most depressing, it was suddenly announced there was a change to fine weather with a high pressure system coming our way. Our prayers had been answered: This was the news we had been waiting for and now it was all systems go.

It was agreed that George and Kath would organise the cutting of the brobs (laurel bushes) on the Silverdale side of the bay but I believe the task of finding these proved to be a bit of a problem for them so rhododendrons were to be used instead. These were plentiful in the grounds of the St John of God's Hospital, Silverdale, where permission to cut them was readily given.

Now, with the better weather prospects I decided that we could start work a day earlier than I had previously anticipated so my helpers had to be notified. I started the week by leading two organised parties from Silverdale to Kents Bank on Saturday May 25th and Sunday May 26th and with other engagements and interviews which I had already promised to fulfil, the week looked like being a pretty hectic one.

A couple of days before the Royal Crossing there were lots of incoming calls to Guides Farm from the press and also this was the first day that the sands and the Kent Channel on the Silverdale side of the bay showed signs of improvement.

I had decided to meet up with my helpers and also Barbara Stothart and her brother, Judge Sandy Temple,

Willing helpers leaving the Silverdale foreshore to mark out the route for the royal carriage crossing. (Bill Gladwin)

both carriage drivers, who offered to come along and look at the route. They finished up giving us a hand as well as Ian Brodie, a teacher and freelance journalist from Garstang, whom I know so well as he has crossed the bay many times under my guidance. He eventually left us behind preparing the route, as he made his first solo crossing of the bay to pick up his car at Guides Farm.

There have been times when I could have taken many more horse-drawn carriages across the sands without problems but for this occasion I saw the bay at the Silverdale side as the most difficult I have known it. To have taken twenty carriages across the bay would have been very difficult- in fact, in a way, I was relieved when the final number of twelve was given to me, bearing in mind the over-all width these carriages would take when spread out, as I did not want anyone following in the tracks of the others in front on the first half and most dangerous part of their journey.

It took us two days to mark out the route from the Silverdale side using two hundred brobs from rhododendron bushes to a point almost half way across the bay where the sand rose to a higher level and was safe and sound. Many of the brobs had to be replaced after each tide as the river Kent moved its course. The route chosen was not straight across but snaked to and fro to avoid large areas of shifting sands. This also added to the mileage which was approximately six miles.

No more could be done at this stage from the Silverdale side as it was now Wednesday evening and we had yet to travel back to Grange.

I then had to find a good friend with lots of laurels, who would allow us to cut them for the purpose of marking out the route on the Grange-over-Sands side of the bay. Mrs E. Williams of Kents Bank came to the rescue. It was not long before we had enough cut and bundled, all ready for an early start, very early, out into the bay from Grange side on my old tractor.

On the night of May 29th I went to bed to sleep knowing that I had done everything humanly possible to make the crossing for His Royal Highness and friends pleasureable, and above all safe.

It would be to our advantage to make an early start on the morning of May 30th 1985 along with my helpers, son-in-law, Chris, and John Barber a friend of mine. We set out from Guides Farm at 3.30 am. over sands which I knew well, but carefully choosing the route so that markers could be put in the sand on the return journey. The first priority was to get out there to the river Kent for what was to be the final check before the Royal Carriage Drive across the sands in the afternoon following the next tide. You would never believe a river could behave in such a way! It had moved at least one hundred and fifty yards away from the markers put in the sand only the day before. What I did not realise until we were in the river testing the sand for firmness was that it had improved itself and moved onto a bed of much firmer sand. I was more satisfied now than I had ever been before. All we had to do now was to move some of the original markers and replace the ones which had been washed away. Then we turned for home, putting what were now small laurel branches to complete the route all the way back to Kents Bank Station. The day dawned with a clear sky and as we watched the sun rise, we knew then that we were in for a perfect day.

I was feeling a bit tired when we arrived back at Guides Farm so I decided to have a rest for a couple of hours. I did not want to be half asleep for the drive across the sands in the afternoon. It was not long though before the silence was broken by a barrage of telephone calls from the press. These were continuous and went on well into the afternoon. It is not unusual for us to receive lots of calls at the farm, mostly about the walks over the sands but we had never known anything like this before. There was just no break from one call to the next. Lots of local people and even coach operators from as far as Morecambe and Blackpool telephoned with enquiries as to where I would be bringing the Duke of Edinburgh ashore. Excitement started early in the day not only with the telephone calls but people were calling at the door. One woman, Mrs

Leah, from Cart Lane, ninety-two years young and still driving her own car came to the Farm to see us. She wanted to know whether it would be possible for people to sit on the seats which are situated on the way down to the foreshore just across from the railway station, at Kents Bank and would the police allow this….I had been told at a meeting earlier that the place alloted to the public was to be a roped off area down on the sands and also that vehicles would not be allowed to park along the roadside near to the station in Kentsford Road. I just conveyed that message to everyone who asked these questions. Mrs Leah was so determined to find out for herself, that she made several visits to Kents Bank. She even took with her her own little folding chair, went down onto the sands and sat down, looked around and decided that she was too low down. She then came back onto the station platform, but then she sat down and found she could not see anything but the wall. She said to herself, "this is no good, what next". She then drove along to a friend in Kents Bank whose house overlooks the bay with magnificent views and was told in conversation that they were having tea on the lawn and would watch the carriage crossing of the sands from there and invited her to stay. This was nice she thought, but no! she was determined to be there on the shore at Kents Bank to see for herself H.R.H., The Duke of Edinburgh,and all the other horses and their drivers, not forgetting the beautiful Shire horses from Tetley Walkers. So she declined her friend's kind offer.

Although the drive was not due to leave the far side of the bay until 3.30pm., Mrs Leah decided to take a chance, and get down to Kents Bank Station by twelve noon.On arrival she noticed that people had already started to park their cars along the side of the roadway to Kents Bank Station so naturally she did the same. As she crossed the railway she also saw to her amazement that people were already sitting on the seats which I had previously told her they would not be allowed to do.There was just room for her so she squeezed herself in along with her flask of coffee, her sandwiches and of course her camera.

Meanwhile, back at the farm, all was bustling with activity. My wife, Olive and daughter Jean were baking and preparing lots of nice things. They had decided to lay on a buffet for our helpers and friends,when we all met back there after the sands crossing.

There were so many representatives from the press, world wide in fact, that it was arranged that I would supply two tractors and trailers and one pick-up truck to transport some of these people across the sands to a safe area where they could stop and wait with their cameras at the ready. I had decided on the place, and as I was not going to be along with them, this had to be a safe one. This was now going to be the responsibility of my son-in-law, Chris, and friends John Barber and Larry Bennett. After giving them a little advice and wishing them well, I now had to think about getting myself round to the other side of the bay, to Silverdale. I was extremely lucky. Some friends whom we hadn't seen for years, gave us what they thought at first was to be a flying visit. When we told them of the carriage crossing, they both offered to stay and help in any way possible. Jaqueline was soon busy, helping Olive with the cleaning and dusting, and making sandwiches, whilst her husband Geoff offered to take me round to Silverdale in his car. I was feeling relaxed now and kissed Olive good-bye before making down the pathway to our transport. Everyone wished me well and we were soon on our way. I always carry my stick with me when testing the sands on the organised walks but today for the first time, I left it behind. On purpose of course. Instead, on this occcasion I carried with me a coastguard walkie-talkie and am pleased to say that I had no need to use this.

My friend Geoff was familiar with the A6 road but had never driven in the Silverdale area. Whichever way we decided on meant narrow country roads with many bends. Luckily I decided that we turn off the A6 at Beetham and then make for Silverdale as we heard later that the Arnside to Silverdale was so congested with traffic that the police had great difficulty in dealing with this problem. As we drove through the village and down towards the shore road, at a place where the road divides, there were policemen stopping all traffic. We could hear quite plainly what they were saying to the drivers in front of us 'No more parking down on the shore, but there is a car park just opened up, a little way down on the left'. As we followed the vehicles in front of us we found that Dick had opened up a field to the public for the day, and what a good idea.

On seeing Dick, Geoff and I were directed away from the other vehicles, and were able to park near to Dick's house. He was so pleased to see us and along with his family and friends everyone was so excited. The first thing he said to me was "Does ta want a cup a tea to calm thi nerves Ced". I thanked him for the kind offer, but I thought it was time for us to be making our way down and across the marsh towards the Cove. "Isn't a nervous" then Dick said "Look at me". He was shaking like a leaf!

A few days earlier, I was asked by a T.V. Company who were interested in filming the carriage drive over the sands from a helicopter if it was safe to land their machine on the marsh as near to the Cove as possible without it being in the way of the horses and carriages at the start of the drive. I agreed to their request and I arranged that a friend of mine would be at the spot on the day with a white flag, to guide the pilot and his machine into position. This friend was Dick Proctor, who was to be the flagman and this was the reason for his nervousness. He had told me earlier that he had made himself a flag and that he would wear something that would make him clearly visible from the air. "Wont be a minute" he said to us, as he opened up the door of an outbuilding and stepped inside. He soon reappeared, carrying his home-made flag. This was a broomstick with lots of white material tied to it. He wore a thick, vivid orange-coloured waistcoat and looked like a council cum lollipop man. "How do ah luck" he said, "Will ah do?" We couldn't help laughing, but this was all taken in good part. Dick was looking forward to this responsible job and now said "Well, wi better bi gy'n or

will miss yon pilot". So we made our way down onto the foreshore and found large numbers of people basking in the glorious sunshine. The little picturesque village must never have known such activity as thousands of people had flocked down to the foreshore to catch a glimpse of the Duke. Most of them had gathered in Silverdale several hours before the Duke had even arrived. The village was virtually taken over for the day as families filled the main street and cars were jammed along most roads… It proved a day out for all the family, their pets and what seemed like most of the village's large community of senior citizens.

One senior citizen, Mary Holmes, whom I know quite well, was Mary Dickinson before her marriage and is now a widow in her eighties though she looks much younger. She has lived in one of the shore cottages since she was two years old and as a young girl used to follow the sands with her father, John Dickinson. On the days of the Cross Bay walks when time permitted I would call on her and she was always so pleased as she loved to talk about the sands and her memories of them. It was sad to hear from Dick Proctor that she had been taken ill and was now in a Private Nursing Home in the village. I still visited her there and she seemed pretty strong and when I had confirmation of the carriage drive with the Duke of Edinburgh taking part, I called and gave the Manager of the Home and Mary, of course, the details of the drive and thought "Wouldn't it be nice if Mary and others who were able could be taken down to the foreshore to see this spectacle for themselves"?

By now we were mingling with the crowds, and it would have been very difficult to see anyone you knew unless you actually bumped into them. Dick was now feeling a bit uneasy as we were still quite a long way from the Cove area when two helicopters came circling overhead and eventually landed some distance from us at the the end of the marsh near to the sands. He now thought he would be better making over towards them and inquiring into what was happening. So here it was that we parted company and we did not see him again that day.

Meanwhile Geoff and I were now following a route which had been marked with short white painted wooden pegs.

These were in a continuous line almost parallel with the Shoreline from the Cove towards the cottages to meet up with the old cockle road. This was a fairly uneven route to my mind but there seemed to be no alterative. There was nothing the Silverdale people would have liked better than to have seen the Duke of Edinburgh and his magnificent team and the other's carriages drive along the road and down through the village and onto the shore. The police said they could not guarantee maximum security to cover this so it was decided right from the start that an alternative had to be found.

Quite large crowds had gathered on the shore in the Cove area and as we passed close to a policeman we could hear quite plainly over his walkie-talkie that the Duke had arrived at Stone Bower.

It was at this point that a man came out to us from the crowd holding a copy of my latest book, "One Man's Morecambe Day", and after introducing himself he said he had brought the book with him just on the chance of meeting me. He asked if I would kindly put my signature in it for him. I obliged and he thanked me very much and wished me luck on the trip across the bay.

We were now just leaving the shore and about to open the gate into Cove Lane when suddenly we heard the noise of another helicopter coming up the bay towards Silverdale. We now thought of Dick and wondered how he had gone on. This must be the 'copter that would be on the lookout for him. As we watched it circled above the marsh and then landed alongside the other two. It was now only a matter of minutes before we should be in the grounds of Stone Bower. The narrow Cove Lane was packed with people on both sides.

Some of them were sitting on the walls to get a better view and everyone looked so happy on this most beautiful sunny day. As we turned left at the top of the lane a policeman was standing there on duty. I said to Geoff as we approached "I hope this copper recognises me and allows us both through". Geoff was carrying a camera so we were really surprised as we both strolled past him and he did not say one word. He just stared almost through us and I thought if looks could kill both Geoff and I would now be stone dead: The look on his face was so noticeable especially after seeing all the happy crowds around us. Talking about happy people Mr Bernard Wood, the manager of the Home at Stone Bower, and all the patients were so pleased when it was agreed that the organised drive was to start from their grounds.

As the horse-boxes were arriving, the one carrying the Duke's magnificent Cleveland Bays was allowed by the security men to be parked as near as possible to the Home. This was to allow the patients to watch the preparations, such as grooming, harnessing etc.

As we entered the grounds, two security men beckoned us over and said with a smile, "Mr Robinson, they are all ready and waiting for you in the paddock". We could now see all the drivers, including H.R.H., sitting up in their carriages waiting at the ready. It was here that Geoff and I had to part company. Mr Lea, from Holker Hall, was standing alongside the Duke's carriage and gave me a wave so I made my way over towards him. "Hello Mr Robinson" he said "Please climb aboard". I remembered that it had been agreed upon that on the day of the drive I would give a briefing to all the drivers just prior to moving out from Stone Bower. This, to my mind was an essential part of the safety of this drive. Mr Lea then asked all the drivers if they would kindly step down from their carriages and gather round. I had nothing planned of what I was going to say, but this I felt needed to be plain and simple and as short as possible. There were a few worried faces looking my way so I thought I would give them a little reassurance. First I told them that the drive was not going to be dangerous and that we were going out there to enjoy ourselves. "It is something different and will certainly be a great experience" I said. I then had to look at the number of horses to each carriage, then quickly weigh up in my mind which order I should put them in to suit the conditions out there in the bay. This could then be put into practice as soon as we reached the sands. I decided that I would like them to line up in two groups of six, side by side, but allowing a safe distance between the carriages. The Duke's carriage would be on the right flank of the front line, and the second line of six would follow at least fifty yards behind to the left of us, as this would help us to eliminate any danger through the areas of softer sand. I thought this order should be kept also until we were at least half way across the bay and clear of the low-lying, watery areas. Once we reached the higher ground the sands would be much firmer and quite safe so that we could then follow one carriage behind the other just slightly offset in the same way the fishermen used to do, including myself, when we followed the sands with horse and cart.

The time had now come, when all drivers and their passengers were to climb aboard their carriages. The groomsmen had been minding the horses meanwhile and these horses were all immaculately turned out.

I was asked to climb up on the front seat and sit along-side H.R.H., The Duke of Edinburgh.

The drive started at 3.30 pm., with the Prince leading the procession, flanked by policemen on horseback.

The Prince was in charge of a team of four magnificent Cleveland Bays, and behind came eleven other carriages with two outriders bringing up the rear.

All but one of the patients at Stone Bower were brought outside to watch this great event. This was to be the experience of their lifetime.

Harvey Burrows, the oldest patient in the Home came from Silverdale. He was not able to join the other patients outside but was not to miss the event altogether though. It was decided that he should be taken to the top of the fire escape where he would get a bird's eye view. All the patients in the Home are elderly and they really got something out of this event. It would be a talking point for weeks to come. It was such a wonderful day too, with the sun shining down on everyone. It could even be said that this event brought a little sunshine into their lives, by giving them all much pleasure and a memorable day, as they watched the cavalcade move out of the grounds of Stone Bower, slowly to disappear into the distance down Cove Lane towards the sands. Large crowds lined the route with everyone cheering and clapping as the Duke's carriage came into view. Cameras were clicking from all angles. From where I was sitting it looked as if everyone who could hold a camera had brought one along with them on this beautiful day.

Watching H.R.H. handle his team, one sensed the power and intelligence of these four Cleveland Bays as the Duke spoke frequently to them, calling each one of them by its name as we made our way down to the shore. This took us only a matter of minutes. Here again large crowds had gathered on the marsh and it was here that we lost the route at the start. I soon realised the mistake and pointed this out to the Duke. Luckily, amongst the crowds of people and all the parked cars was a space wide enough to allow H.R.H. to manoeuvre his team around and pick up the route. All the other drivers followed in single file. People who were standing in that area were obscuring our view of the small white wooden pegs which had been put in as markers and, as the marsh was a jigsaw of gullies, it was not easy to pick out the route.

On the most awkward and narrow drain-offs, the organisers had laid planks of wood to prevent any of the horses getting a leg down into one these. As we approached the first one, I instinctively held on to the side of the carriage thinking to myself "I know what is going to happen here, the horses will jump this". They did, but after negotiating the first one they took the others in their stride, as the Duke spoke quietly to them on the approach. Then they just walked on, ignoring the boards and the crowds around them. It was more than I could say for some of the other horses following behind. I believe that some of the drivers had great difficulty in getting their teams to cross these boards as the horses kept rearing and almost upturned the carriages.

Sir Sandy Temple, accompanied by his wife, and Lord Cavendish of Holker Hall at the start of the royal carriage drive. (Barbara Stothart)

Eventually, we were all on much firmer ground and near to the sands, when three very noisy helicopters were flying overhead, and at this stage seemed to upset the horses a little more.

The helicopters had been hired by the media to take aerial shots of the Duke in action on the Cross Bay drive.

Ahead now, lining both sides of the track we were following, was the largest crowd of people I have ever seen and they reached right along to where the marsh met up with the sands. Once we had all arrived in this area it was here that the drivers would line up their horses and carriages in the order that I had suggested at the briefing.

From here onwards the sands route was very clearly marked with brobs (laurel branches) and for the first half of the drive would make it easier for the drivers to follow with two rows of brobs leaving the width between the only safe route. It was here that the difficulty arose as the spectators surged down onto the sands following the Duke's carriage. Lots of people ran into the path of the horses and when we drew to a halt for a few moments it seemed chaotic. I could only see two other carriages as they came forward to the line-up. One was being driven by Judge Sandy Temple from Yealand and his passenger was Lord Hugh Cavendish of Holker Hall. The driver of the other carriage was Mrs Barbara Stothert, sister of Judge Temple. The others were completely lost in the crowds and now this was going to cause us a delay. It was here that I asked the Duke whether he would mind if I stepped down from the carriage to help the mounted police with the crowds. It was not easy at first because there were just too many people who had closed in, in order to get a better view of the Duke and a few shots with their cameras. Some even came so close as to stroke the horses!!

Eventually, the crowds responded to our requests for them to move back towards the marsh, and enable the other carriages to come through and line up ready for the OFF.

This took only a matter of minutes and as soon as I could see that everyone was ready, Prince Philip told his

team of horses to walk on and the drive across the sands had begun. Cheers went up as we left the crowds behind and soon the horses were asked to trot on. It was not easy here for the carriage drivers as you can imagine but two coast-guard vehicles were on hand to make sure none of the enthusiastic crowd wandered too far out onto the sands.

Nothing had been rehearsed and with horses of different sizes and temperament they had difficulty at first in keeping their distances and at times were far too close for comfort. As we progressed out into the bay the drivers became accustomed to it and the horses all seemed to be enjoying it too.

The river Kent was crossed at a trot as the river was fast flowing and axle deep, but it was here that one of the lead horses pulling the Royal carriage, decided that he did not like the look of one of my brobs in the river and shied away rather sharply to the left but a word from the Duke soon straightened him up. These Clevelands were very powerful horses but the Duke, being the splendid horseman he is, controlled them with his quietly spoken commands. I found it quite an experience watching the Duke handle his team.

Where the route was marked clearly it was possible for me to look around and keep an eye on the other carriages to see how they were doing. Shortly after the river crossing there was another stretch of water slightly deeper but with less flow than the main river. Also this stretch deepened fairly sharply away over to the left and shelved off. My worry here was that if the smallest pony on the drive, a grey Welsh mountain pony just over eleven hands high were to be on the left of the other carriages he would have found that he had to swim. Looking back over my shoulder I saw that he was in amongst the other horses and doing well with neck outstretched. I think here though that the drivers and passengers would have got a little wetting.

It was here that I was able to describe to H.R.H. about the river and its movements and also about the quicksands. He was interested and I found him very easy to talk to. I had to ask H.R.H. to slow the pace of his powerful team as we were leaving the other carriages with smaller horses and ponies well behind.

At one time the helicopters came in too close and I could almost feel the carriage shoot from under us as this seemed to upset the horses a little but again the Duke spoke reassuringly to his team and they soon settled down.

I was now just beginning to feel more relaxed as everything seemed to be going well and I was enjoying the ride. Ahead of us was one more stretch of water which until recently had been the river Kent. This was wide but shallow, and on the far bank awaiting H.R.H. and the cavalcade of of horse-drawn vehicles was the media, there to capture the first story and pictures of such a crossing for over a century.

Our approach to this was in wide formation with the horses now moving briskly at the trot. As I looked from the carriage to my left along the whole line of turn-outs I thought what a wonderful sight this was to see as they all entered the water at the same time trying hard to keep in formation. This began to bring back happy memories to me of shrimping with horse and cart as I heard the horses hooves pounding through the water and the swish of the carriage wheels going round.

Very soon we were all clear and out on the other side travelling over what was now good firm sand. From here on, at about half way across the bay the horses were asked to slow to walking pace, and it was now possible for the carriages to follow one behind the other. The sand rose up here to a much higher level and with a combination of much lower tides, a dry warm breeze and brilliant sunshine, the views around were so clear that we were now looking at the bay at its best. It was here that the drivers took the opportunity to relax their concentration and take in the sweeping panorama of this beautiful bay. I also took the opportunity to chat with the Duke as I was so taken up with his team. I asked him questions about the horses and he answered them. He chatted freely and asked me questions about the bay and the route we were taking.

We still had the company of the helicopters flying overhead and away to our left were the tractors and trailers carrying the press photographers. There were also several other vehicles including a pick-up truck, a coastguard land rover and a beach buggy which had travelled out into the bay from Cannibal Island, at Kents Bank.

As the Duke now told his team to trot on, I was hoping that we would not arrive at Kents Bank Station before our time. Negotiations with British Rail to ensure maximum safety over the railway crossing had resulted in their agreement to lay boards over the railway lines where the horses and carriages were to cross after the 4.15 passenger train had left the station.

Occasionally the pace slowed down as dykes and gullies were crossed but as the Royal cavalcade came into view of the thousands who had gathered on the foreshore at Kents Bank to witness the occasion, the team of Shire horses belonging to Tetley Walkers, Brewers, the sponsors of this drive, were waiting to be driven in the procession behind the Duke's leading carriage. It was agreed that from here to the Shore all the horses would come in at a steady trot.

By now lots of people were running alongside with their cameras to take shots of the Duke and at one stage, a young boy on a bicycle rode straight into the path of the Duke's horses. Sweeping this minor annoyance aside the Duke seemed in high spirits.

As we now approached the large crowds towards the end of this historic crossing cheers went up and H.R.H. spoke to me saying "Stand up, Mr Robinson, it's you they are cheering, not me." I didn't, though the atmosphere, with everyone looking so happy and in carnival mood with the brass band playing as the Royal Carriage pulled up at Kents Bank gave me this unbelievable feeling. It really filled me up inside.

We had conquered the bay with its unpredictable moods and quicksands. This was certainly the most memorable day of my life.

The Duke hereby doffed his cap and remarked on the trip as delightful apart from the noise of the helicopters,

(Below) The Duke of Edinburgh and Cedric Robinson at Kent's Bank station after crossing the Bay. (Westmorland Gazette)
(Opposite) The arrival at Kent's Bank. (Barrow News & Mail)

and that he had complete faith in his Guide.

It was now time for the local dignatories to meet the Duke, followed by a presentation by Tetley Walkers Limited, of an inscribed glass tankard to commemorate the Kent Sands crossing by horse-drawn Carriages. As the Duke was presented with the tankard, he immediately inquired if there was one for me. As there was only one he decided to give me his. I was surprised but also very pleased and thanked him very much.

The time had come now to move off with the horses and cross the railway over the newly laid boards. As the Duke drove now on the road past the Kents Rank Post Office, he chose to halt his team of horses under the shade of some trees near to Priory Lane. I now climbed down from the Royal Carriage, my assignment being completed, and made my way to the Kents Bank Hotel to meet up with my friends. It was question time for the press, and then it was home for me to my wife Olive, our family and friends, to have our own little celebration.

After the bay crossing there were the Horse Trials at Holker Hall and Park to which Olive and I went. We were standing at the back of a crowd of people when the Duke of Edinburgh passed. He caught sight of us and waved, calling to us "Have you recovered from the ordeal, Mr Robinson"?

To add to the appreciation of the successful sands crossing, one week later I received a letter of warm thanks from Lady Cavendish saying "The crossing was a wonderful success, and a magical experience".

On June 13th Olive and I were invited to have lunch at Holker Hall with the Cavendish family and Mr Lea, which we were very pleased to accept and greatly enjoyed.

Another very nice surprise for us was to receive, the following day, a kind letter of thanks from Buckingham Palace.

The participants for the Kent crossing were as follows:-

1. H.R.H. The Duke of Edinburgh driving a team of four horses to a marathon vehicle
2. Mrs B. Stothert driving a single horse to a Liverpool gig made in 1897
3. Judge E.S. Temple driving a cob to a Dog Cart
4. Mr G. Denney driving a single horse to a marathon vehicle
5. Mr M. Broadbent driving a team of four ponies to a Phoenix Champion marathon Vehicle
6. Mrs E. Craig driving a Welsh pony to an exercise cart
7. Mrs C. Dickens driving a single horse to a Ralli Cart
8. Mr J. Richards driving a team of four horses to a Kuhnle marathon vehicle
9. Mrs A. Winn driving ponies in tandem
10. Mr K. Scowcroft driving a pair of horses to a marathon vehicle
11. Mrs F. Milner driving a Baby Bennington Buggy.

SPECIAL ANNIVERSARY

1999 marked the 600th Anniversary of the link between the Duchy of Lancaster and the Crown. In 1399, Henry Bolinbroke, Duke of Lancaster, became Henry IV and the Duchy has been held by the Sovereign ever since.

To commemorate the 600th Anniversary, a service in the Priory Church at Lancaster was to take place in the presence of Her Majesty the Queen, Duke of Lancaster and His Royal Highness The Prince Philip, Duke of Edinburgh, on Friday 23rd July, 1999 at 11a.m, for which I was invited to apply for a ticket to the service. One ticket only could be issued for security reasons, so I could not take my wife, Olive, along with me. More detailed arrangements would be sent to me with the ticket in July.

Following the Church Service, the Royal Luncheon was to be held in the Town Hall, Lancaster, to which I was also invited.

The invitations were strictly private and confidential for security reasons, and although my wife, Olive and I were thrilled and excited about receiving these invitations we had to adhere to the rules untill after the event. We did not even discuss this with any of our own close family,

The greatest surprise was to find that I would be sitting on Top Table 2, along with H.R.H.The Duke of Edinburgh and many other famous people including Mrs Joan Bartholemew, the widow of that late great comedian, Eric Morecambe.

The Queen, on the morning of July 23rd, had been in the town of Morecambe to unveil the statue of the late Eric Morecambe, overlooking the view of that magical place, Morecambe Bay.

The statue of Eric Morecambe after unveiling by the Queen. (Lancaster & Morecambe Newspapers)

KNOCKING KNEES AT BUCKINGHAM PALACE

The Dawn Chorus is my alarm clock during the Spring and Summer mornings and this usually starts at around 6 am and continues till 6.30 am. I am used to rising early and coming downstairs to put the kettle on to make a brew for Olive, my wife, which I then take up to her, come down and have my drink and wait for the postman, who usually comes around 7.30. I then go through the stream of mail.

This particular morning, 6th May 1999, seemed at first to be like the start of any other morning until one letter I noticed stood out from the others and written in bold letters was "FROM NO 10 DOWNING STREET LONDON" and marked Confidential.

When I opened the letter I just could not believe it. I was so excited I ran upstairs to show Olive and let her read it for herself.

Olive, after reading the letter was also extremely pleased but she did say not to build too much into this as H. M. The Queen would have to agree with the Prime Minister's recommendation, so we did not tell a soul, not even close family.

The Prime Minister, in the forthcoming list of Birthday Honours, was to submit my name to The Queen with a recommendation that Her Majesty may approve that I be appointed a Member of the Order of the British Empire. Before doing so and with my agreement I was to complete a form which was enclosed and send it by return post. Then, if the Queen accepted the Prime Minister's recommendation the announcement would be made in the Birthday Honours' List.

This was published on 12th June 1999 and my name was included.

Copies of the Honours' List were to be given to the Press, Radio and Television organisations. I received a Telemessage from H.R.H. The Duke of Edinburgh congratulating me on my well deserved honour and another very nice letter from Buckingham Palace written by the Lady-in-Waiting to Princess Alexandra, who was asked to send her congratulations to me. I was privileged to have met Princess Alexandra at lunch at Lancaster University when I was given an honorary degree in 1996.

Included in the letters of congratulations was one from James Cropper F.C.A. of Tolson Hall, Kendal, who is Lord Lieutenant of Cumbria. Also an almost endless list of people who, after hearing the announcement on the radio and T.V., very kindly put pen to paper and offered their congratulations to me on this achievement. We also received lots of lovely cards for which we were both grateful. I should also mention the very good people who thought I was worthy to be nominated for this honour.

No date was given to me for the investiture at Buckingham Palace at this stage but as time went on friends would ask "When are you going down to London for your gong, Cedric"!! Eventually all details arrived through the post and the big day was to be Thursday, 2nd December 1999.

Throughout the summer we were so busy with the bay walks that I hardly had time to think about the trip to London, or even to wonder how we were going to get there.

Some very good friends of ours, Geoff and Jackie, who live in Worcester come to stay in the caravan park at Meathop, near Grange-over-Sands each year for a break and when they knew of our visit to the Palace, they insisted on taking us there by road in their minibus.

They very kindly suggested that we should be ready

Cedric chats with the Queen after receiving the MBE in December 1999.

and waiting to be picked up on Tuesday, 30th November 1999 about mid-day, staying at their home for two nights. This short break was just what Olive and I needed. Then we would get up early on the Thursday morning about 4.30a.m. I think it was, to leave their house no later than 6.00a.m. for our journey to London.

We arrived at the Palace Gates at about 10.15a.m., joining a queue of vehicles waiting as each one had to be checked before driving through the Main Archway into the Palace Grounds. All the drivers of the vehicles were asked not to lock their car doors. As we stepped out into the inner courtyard the weather seemed pretty cold and a breeze, which did not help as Olive, against her will was persuaded by many friends to wear a hat on this occasion. They said "Oh! You will have to wear a hat, everyone wears a hat on this special occasion". So knowing Olive, she went along with this hat idea but was not really happy and this made her nervous.

As the four of us approached the main entrance to the Palace and walked slowly up the thickly carpeted steps, military personnel were placed at intervals to show the way and there were also signs which were plain to see. At the top of the stairway an arrowed sign read 'Recipients this way' and 'Guests the other'. As we parted company Olive and our good friends Geoff and Jackie wished me luck and then I needed to use the toilets and made a beeline for the Gents!

By gum! Were they posh! All the taps were highly polished in gold.

I was now feeling nervous – a bit like a fish out of water – as I followed other recipients along into the waiting area which was described as the Picture Gallery and where we were all briefed eventually on the procedure for the day.

I looked around at the recipients to see if there were any familiar faces. Out of the crowd came one person, a woman with a Birmingham accent and she asked me where I had come from. This broke the ice so to speak and she said how nervous she felt and did I feel the same. I certainly did, but it helped when she spoke to me and she said she thought most people here today would be feeling the same way.

I suppose that everyone of the Queen's subjects in fact dreams that one day in their lives they will meet the Queen. Well! I must admit that I was one of those people but never thought it would happen.

There are twenty investitures held each year at Buckingham Palace for the recipients and their guests and this would probably be the first time in their lives when they would be·received by the Queen.

The investiture was held in the Palace Ballroom and started promptly at 11a.m. I was more nervous now than ever before and I almost went deaf with noises in my head.

I was told later that this was caused through anxiety.

As your name was called out you fell in line with about twenty other recipients. It was now a case of watching the person in front of you and when your name was called to go before the Queen. Hopefully you remembered what to do after following the person in front.

I was a bag of nerves and my knees were knocking but as soon as the Queen spoke to me she put me at ease by speaking of my own subject, Morecambe Bay sands.

For many, this was a very exciting experience, but for others, nerve-wracking! But the Queen – she's WONDERFUL! And I felt humbly proud to be one of her subjects.

As evidence for this incredible experience, I have obtained a video of my part in this event and can relive it on the screen and prove to my family and friends that it was not just a dream.

~ ACKNOWLEDGEMENTS ~

My thanks go out to the following who have contributed towards this publication:

Joan Heath and her son Nigel, who is a computer expert — personal thanks for long and enduring patience and making an excellent job of the typescript.

Fred Broomfield

My sisters Jean Sawrey and Peggy Hopper

My dad, Bill Robinson

Clifford and Carol Law

John Wilson of Leighton Moss

Andrew Fairey — Guide's Farm meadow species

Alec Moore, coxswain of Barrow lifeboat

Susannah Bleakley and Louisa — The Morecambe Bay Partnership

Thomas Park Benson

Group Captain Harry King, OBE

Barbara Stothard

I also sincerely thank my wife Olive for helping me in my research and for the contribution of her line drawings to illustrate the text.